Players and personalities featured in GRAND SLAM:

Alvin Davis
Todd Worrell
Andy Van Slyke
Glenn Davis
Bobby Meacham
Jesse Barfield
Lloyd Moseby

Jim Gantner
Lance Parrish
Storm Davis
Orel Hershiser
Andre Thornton
Branch Rickey
Jackie Robinson

**Foreword and Special Section by
Bobby Richardson**

GRAND SLAM

HEROES OF MAJOR LEAGUE BASEBALL

Bill Horlacher & Joe Smalley

Here's Life Publishers

Published by
HERE'S LIFE PUBLISHERS, INC.
P. O. Box 1576
San Bernardino, CA 92402-1576

HLP Product No. 951715
©1987, Bill Horlacher and Joe Smalley
All rights reserved.

Printed in the United States of America.

Library of Congress Cataloging-in-Publication Data

Horlacher, Bill.
  Grand slam.

    1. Baseball players — United States — Biography.
2. Baseball — Religious aspects — Christianity.
I. Smalley, Joe. II. Title.
GV865.A1H64   1987   796.357'092'2 [B]   87-30
ISBN 0-89840-173-9 (pbk.)

Back cover photo of authors by Gray Williams.

Unless otherwise indicated, Scripture quotations are from
the New American Standard Bible, ©The Lockman Foundation 1960, 1962, 1963, 1968, 1972, 1973, 1975, 1977.

FOR MORE INFORMATION, WRITE:

L.I.F.E. — P.O. Box A399, Sydney South 2000, Australia
Campus Crusade for Christ of Canada — Box 300, Vancouver, B.C., V6C 2X3, Canada
Campus Crusade for Christ — Pearl Assurance House, 4 Temple Row, Birmingham, B2 5HG, England
Campus Crusade for Christ — P.O. Box 240, Colombo Court Post Office, Singapore 9117
Lay Institute for Evangelism — P.O. Box 8786, Auckland 3, New Zealand
Great Commission Movement of Nigeria — P.O. Box 500, Jos, Plateau State Nigeria, West Africa
Campus Crusade for Christ International — Arrowhead Springs, San Bernardino, CA 92414, U.S.A.

Contents

Foreword
By Bobby Richardson

I needed a book like this in the mid-1950s. I was in the minor leagues then, a long way from the thrills of playing in eight World Series with such New York Yankee teammates as Mickey Mantle, Roger Maris and Whitey Ford.

My days in the minor leagues were filled with insecurity. There was no aura of greatness; there were no massive stadiums, no lofty salaries. Instead, there were bus exhaust fumes, mediocre hotels and the struggles of trying to make the big leagues.

I still remember arriving in Norfolk, Virginia, site of my first Yankee farm club, at 5 A.M. on a cold, cloudy day in 1953. Left behind were all my friends and supporters. Ahead was a big skeptical world that had seen many a local star fall flat on his face. I was just a green kid, scared of playing with experienced, older men.

My play at Norfolk was terrible, bad enough that the Yankees assigned me to a lower farm team. I began to do better then, but I still faced three long years of apprenticeship in Binghamton, New York; Richmond, Virginia; and Denver before I reached New York.

It's because of the difficulties I faced in the minors that I know a book like *Grand Slam* would have helped me. Its dramatic stories of Christian ballplayers would have encouraged me and shown me that God cared about my problems. Unfortunately, very few outspoken Christians appeared on major league baseball rosters back then — certainly not enough to make a book like this possible. I did, however, receive a helpful letter from my hometown coach, Conley Alexander, who encouraged me to continue in the Christian faith which I had begun a few years before. I still remember that he quoted the words of Matthew 6:33, ". . . seek first His kingdom and His righteousness; and all these things shall be added to you."

It was amazing to see how much strength I drew from that one short letter, and I can't help but wonder what an entire book of inspiration and faith would have meant to me. That's why I'm glad to introduce *Grand Slam* to everyone who loves baseball — from Little Leaguers to major leaguers, from fans to managers. I believe those who read this book will find spiritual strength to cope with the alcohol, the drugs, the personal unrest and the family conflicts that are such a threat to our society.

I'm too old to play for the Yankees anymore, except in "old-timer" games, but I'm glad to be on the same team with the men featured in this book. These men, such as Jesse Barfield, Glenn Davis, Lance Parrish and Todd Worrell, have found the same answer to life's problems that I did. They've found a "spiritual grand slam" through the love of God.

Only in recent years have large numbers of major league ballplayers found a spiritual source of strength.

1

A NEW LUSTRE
COMES TO THE DIAMOND

As a baseball player, Billy Sunday was born several generations too early. He had blinding speed but a weak bat, and he could have used today's artificial turf fields to inflate his .250 lifetime batting average. Still, Sunday played in the dead ball era, so his bold base running (84 stolen bases one year) helped win many low-scoring games. "If only he could steal first," said one observer.[1]

One day in 1887, Sunday was drunk and sitting on a Chicago curb with some of his equally drunk White Stocking teammates. Across the street, a group of men and women began playing instruments and singing gospel hymns. A group member invited the ballplayers to Pacific Garden Mission to "hear (former) drunkards tell how they have been saved and girls tell how they have been saved from the red-light district."[2]

Sunday's response? "I arose and said to the boys,

'I'm through, I am going to Jesus Christ. We've come to the parting of the ways.' . . . I turned and left that little group on the corner and walked to the little mission and fell on my knees and staggered out of sin and into the arms of the Savior."[3]

After three additional years in baseball, Sunday entered Christian service and eventually became a traveling evangelist. In fact, he was known as the "Baseball Evangelist," and he often used athletic stories to help relate the gospel. Sunday was the Billy Graham of his day, speaking to more than 100 million people in about 40 years of travel. One pastor described his impact this way: "As the result of the Billy Sunday campaigns — anywhere and everywhere — drunkards became sober, thieves became honest, multitudes of people engaged themselves in the study of the Bible, thousands confessed their faith in Jesus Christ as the Savior of the world . . ."[4]

Sunday exerted a mighty influence over America, but few ballplayers followed his example. Even as late as the 1950s and '60s, according to former Yankee second baseman Bobby Richardson, "It was uncommon . . . for an athlete to take a stand for Christ." Richardson, however, did take that stand while playing for the nation's most publicized ball club.

In the 1964 World Series, for example, Bobby had a record 13 hits and a .406 batting average — but he made two errors, one of which helped set up a grand slam homer by the Cardinals' Ken Boyer. "I'm not happy over those errors," Richardson told reporters. "But I can't get them changed. It's the same in life. There will be some errors. But in life there's a difference. You can put faith in Christ and have your sins washed away."[5]

Richardson proved that a ballplayer certainly could be committed to Christ and outstanding in his game. Known primarily as a hit-and-run man and as a fielder, Richardson made history with his bat in the 1960 World Series. Despite a victory by Pittsburgh in that Series, Bobby achieved a record six runs-batted-in for one game and a record twelve RBIs for the series. For his heroics, he became the only player on a losing team to be voted

Unlimited Potential in action: Carlos Rios (left), a minor league player in the Braves' organization, and major leaguer Dickie Thon lead a clinic in Puerto Rico

PHOTO: JOSE ISMAEL FERNANDEZ

Most Valuable Player for a World Series.

Richardson led Bible studies for some of his Yankee teammates in the early 1960s. His example was followed by some players on the Minnesota Twins who began a Bible study and then, in 1966 or '67, the Twins started the first chapel services in baseball. Pitcher Jim Kaat helped provide key leadership for the Twins, but his own Christian faith owed a lot to the influence of teammate Al Worthington. "Like many athletes, I thought that Christianity was for sissies, girls and elderly ladies," said Kaat. "But in 1964, Al Worthington joined our ball club, and I became impressed with the kind of life he led. The most important thing to him was his faith in Christ . . . Two years later, I made the decision to invite Christ to come into my life. I dared Him to become real and change me. He has never disappointed me."

Shortly after the Twins began holding chapel services, the Chicago Cubs followed suit. Catcher Randy Hundley and shortstop Don Kessinger were key figures in that effort. Two teams had now found a way for their players to hear God's Word in hotels or clubhouses (Sunday schedules usually keep ballplayers from attending regular church services).

But these isolated efforts were still far from the thriving movement that is today called Baseball Chapel. It began in 1972 primarily through the leadership of Watson Spoelstra, a Detroit sportswriter who is now retired. "Even in the 1940s, when I was a sportswriter for the Associated Press, and later for the *Detroit News,*" says Spoelstra, "I think the only time I ever heard God's name in the clubhouses was in cuss words. It still amazes me that today all the major league teams have worship sessions called 'Baseball Chapel.' What amazes me more is that I had something to do with organizing it."

Once a hard drinker, Spoelstra received Christ when his daughter, Ann, suffered a brain hemorrhage. "God, You do something about Ann," he prayed, "and I'll let You do something about me." A few weeks later, Ann was well and doctors were calling her "the miracle girl" — but her father was also a miracle of a changed life.

Spoelstra eventually teamed with Tiger broadcaster Ernie Harwell (a member of Baseball's Hall of Fame and a committed Christian) in beginning chapel services for Detroit's baseball players. But Spoelstra also saw the need to do something for other teams throughout the major leagues. He talked to Commissioner Bowie Kuhn and received backing to start a ministry to all of major league baseball. In 1973, the first full year of Baseball Chapel, 16 teams participated and within a few years, all 26 took part.

The format for these chapels? Baseball Chapel selects a speaker for each Sunday during the season in each ballpark — perhaps a pastor, a Christian businessman, or an athlete or a coach from another sport. The speaker then provides a Bible-based message for separate services held by the visiting and home teams. More recently,

Baseball Chapel has embraced the minor leagues, and chapels now are held for most farm teams. Bobby Richardson succeeded Spoelstra as the president of Baseball Chapel in December of 1982.

Spoelstra always said that Baseball Chapel was 100 percent God's doing, so it is not surprising that the movement has enjoyed success. Hundreds of minor and major leaguers could echo this comment by Jim Gantner: "The speaker clearly related to me the gospel of Jesus Christ. I became a Christian. Now my wife and I both go to Bible study. Thanks to Baseball Chapel for eternally affecting my life."

Baseball Chapel is not alone in ministering to the baseball world. Organizations like Athletes in Action, the Fellowship of Christian Athletes, and Pro Athletes Outreach all reach out to players through personal contact and through conferences. Another ministry, Unlimited Potential, aids the players in proclaiming their faith by holding outreach events in North America and in many foreign nations.

But whatever organization or individual is involved, the same result is always sought — changed lives. And baseball has seen many of them:

●Gary Carter may seem like the kind of person who always wins, who always has things his way. Not so. Carter's mother died of leukemia when he was just 12 years old, and he responded with bitterness toward God. "I couldn't understand why a loving God would take away someone so dear to me," said Carter. "Because of the loss, I stopped going to church and refused to let God have any part of my life." It wasn't until Gary met fellow catcher John Boccabella with the Expos that he also met Christ. "I saw that God didn't hate me or have anything against me. On the contrary, He loved me very much. When I understood that, I asked Jesus Christ to come into my life."[6]

●When the Mets acquired Carter from the Expos in 1985, *Inside Sports* asked him, "What does it mean to you that you're earning so much money, and that you might lead the Mets to a pennant?" Said Carter, "I'm just so thankful to Jesus Christ for the opportunity to play this game. When the time comes when I can absorb all this, it'll be a great feeling. If we can win the World Series the trade will be worthwhile. It was meant to be. If we do win, Jesus is the man I'll be thankful to. All stats and salaries are fine and dandy, but give all the power and glory to Jesus Christ."[7] True to his word, Gary Carter celebrated the 1986 Mets' World Series victory over Boston by giving thanks to Christ.

●Clint Hurdle, a rookie in 1977, made *Sports Illustrated's* cover as "This Year's Phenom." But he found others' expectations impossible to meet. "If I had done everything I was supposed to," said Hurdle in 1978, "I'd be leading the league in homers, have the highest batting average, have given $100,000 to the Cancer Fund and be married to Marie Osmond." Although he never achieved that level of greatness, Hurdle did play on championship teams in Kansas City. "I had it all — a beautiful wife, a $200,000-a-year income, a house on the lake, a house on the golf course, one new car after another. But I was never satisfied."

Hurdle hurt his back in 1981, and later that year his marriage failed and eventually ended in divorce. Fortunately, after reading the Bible and talking with Christian ballplayers, he trusted Christ as his Savior and Lord. Despite several trades and even a brief minor league demotion, Hurdle had peace of mind. His second wife gave birth to a baby girl in 1985, and Clint had this to say: "I know I'll be the best father I can possibly be. I couldn't have said that with conviction a few years ago."

●Bob Knepper claimed to be an atheist during his high school and minor league days. Then, with the San Francisco Giants, he met fellow pitcher Gary Lavelle. "At first I kept telling him how ridiculous it was to believe in God," says Knepper. But as he continued to talk with Lavelle and began to attend chapel services, Knepper questioned his own stand.

One night on a road trip, the former atheist lay awake in bed and began to pray: "God, I don't know if You exist. I may just be talking to the walls. But if You do exist, then I know I need You. I know I am a sinner in Your eyes. If You are real, then I want You as my Savior and Lord." It was an uncertain start, but Knepper's faith grew steadily in fellowship with Lavelle and others. "God showed me just how real He is," says Knepper, who was traded to Houston in 1982 and achieved much success with the Astros.

●Dave Dravecky says he had always been aware of God and of Jesus Christ. He was even appointed assistant chapel leader for a Pittsburgh Pirates farm team. And yet, says Drevecky, "I felt that as long as things were going all right, I didn't need Him because I could take care of things myself."

A trade to the San Diego organization may have caused a little uncertainty, and it also introduced the left-handed hurler to a teammate with Amarillo named Byron Ballard. It was through friendship with Ballard and other Christian players that Dravecky and his wife, Janice, realized their need to trust Christ instead of their own efforts. Before, says Dravecky, "Everything in my life was self-oriented. I was materialistic and putting too much emphasis on statistics. I knew something was missing, but I couldn't pinpoint it."

When he observed in his Christian teammates the very qualities he desired, Dravecky knew he needed the Lord. "I didn't become a Christian to become successful as a pitcher," he says. "My reason — our reason — for accepting Jesus Christ was because we were missing something in our lives and we were not sure of our destiny or life after death."

But even when these and other stories of changed lives are told, some people remain skeptical. "Sure, those baseball players are Christians," they say. "Show me a six-figure salary and I'll pray, too!" But it's in the life-and-death situations that a Christian's faith shows through in a way that skeptics can't deny.

●Who could dispute the reality of Andre Thornton's faith? The Cleveland Indians slugger lost his wife and daughter in an accident on the Pennsylvania Turnpike, October 17, 1977. Even the hospital chaplain who was with Thornton right after the tragedy could hardly believe the man's spiritual strength. "He just wanted me to be with him while he prayed," said the Rev. Wayne Sautter. "What astounded me was that it was totally a prayer of thanksgiving. He thanked God that he had his wife and daughter while he did. He had heartache but also a sense of peace that was unbelievable . . . That man would be a powerful witness to anybody."[8]

●Tommy John and his wife, Sally, demonstrated a similar faith when their little toddler, Travis, fell out of a third-story window during the summer of 1981. Travis was in critical condition for several days, and the Johns' official statement to the public asked "all our friends to pray for Travis's full and healthy recovery."

Travis did recover fully, but even when he first began to improve, his father expressed gratitude to God. "My prayers have been answered," he said. "It looks like he's going to be OK. It's something you wish didn't happen, but it did. All things happen for the glory of God. When we get through this ordeal, my wife, Sally, and I will be stronger as a husband and wife than ever before."

Tommy, of course, was already accustomed to trusting God in seemingly bleak situations. He had torn a ligament in his pitching arm in 1974 and received a transplanted tendon from his opposite wrist as a replacement. Although the surgeon urged Tommy to find another profession, he underwent more than a year of grueling rehabilitation while praying that God would heal his arm.

Regardless of the result, John was ready to trust his loving Lord. "If it hadn't worked out, it would have meant that God had something else in store for me, something better than baseball," he said. To the amazement of baseball experts, Tommy John not only returned to the mound, but his "bionic arm" was a 20-game winner for both the Dodgers and Yankees.

●And then there's the case of Danny Thompson, a shortstop with the Twins and Rangers, whose brief life taught others much about the value of knowing Christ. A routine physical exam in 1973 showed that Thompson had leukemia. During the 1973 season, Thompson made a total commitment of his life to Christ. "I always went to church when I was growing up," said Danny. "I knew all about Jesus Christ. But I never knew God personally. I knew about Him, but I didn't know Him."

Many would have retreated into bitterness or self-pity, but Thompson saw an eternal benefit from his disease. "It's made me a better person," he said. "I really don't have to worry about my future now, because I've turned it over to the Lord."

Thompson played his last season in 1977, seeing action in 98 games for the Twins and Rangers. He died on December 10, 1977, at the age of 28. Baseball Chapel now honors his memory each year by giving the "Danny Thompson Award" to a player who demonstrates strong Christian spirit. Don Kessinger won the first award in 1977, and he was followed by Andre Thornton, Craig Reynolds, Jerry Terrell, Pat Kelly, Geoff Zahn, Gary Lavelle, Jim Essian, Frank Tanana and Clint Hurdle. Said Terrell, a former Twins teammate of Thompson, "It was special to me to receive the award, having known Danny personally. I saw the confidence, peace and assurance that God gave him in his daily battle with leukemia."

You are about to read the inspiring stories of 14 top baseball figures, including Todd Worrell, Glenn Davis, Andre Thornton, Jesse Barfield, Alvin Davis, Andy Van Slyke, Bobby Meacham, Lloyd Moseby, Jim Gantner, Lance Parrish, Storm Davis, and Orel Hershiser. In each chapter you'll get a behind-the-scenes look at the rigors and rewards of professional baseball. You'll be treated to a rare personal glimpse of each individual. Most important, you'll see how each man's personal faith in God has helped him deal with the pressures of the game, and how you, too, can experience the same victory over circumstances in your own life.

This slugger says parents can be cool, too, but who wants Mom for a college roommate?

2

ALVIN DAVIS

Honor Thy Father and Thy Roommate

Ready for a little multiple choice? Scan the list below and choose which of the following you would least like to have as a college roommate:

A. a slob

B. a loud snorer

C. a Heavy Metal fanatic

D. your mother

Pretty tough choice, right? With "A" as a roommate you can't find your stuff. With "B" you can't sleep. With "C" you go deaf. With "D" you go *nowhere*. With your mom as your roommate you're automatically the most uncool person at the university. Sure, you might be the best fed. But who wants to be the best fed and the least cool? Face it. Nobody in his right mind — absolutely *nobody* — chooses his mother as a college roommate.

Don't be so sure. There's at least one guy who did

just that. He plays first base for the Seattle Mariners.
Name's Alvin Davis. He's even cool. It's just that he has
something a lot of guys don't — a great relationship with
his mother.

When Alvin graduated from John W. North High
School in Riverside, California and accepted a scholarship
to Arizona State University, his mother, Mylie, moved
to Tempe, Arizona, with him. Why? Because Alvin talked
her into it. He knew the clean Arizona air would help
with her breathing problem. And Alvin, the youngest
of four boys in the family, had already lived alone with
his mother throughout high school. They were accustomed to each other.

Alvin credits his mother and his faith in Christ as
stabilizing factors that helped him make it to the major
leagues. That happened in 1984. And no one was more
surprised than Davis himself.

In the spring of that year, the Seattle Mariners sent
Alvin back to the minors after barely looking at him
during training camp. The M's already had two left-
handed hitting first basemen and Davis had been a AA
player the year before.

Then regular first baseman Ken Phelps broke his little
finger, and Davis got the call to come back after a grand
total of one game at the AAA level. Manager Del Crandell
lamented Phelps's trip to the disabled list. "It's a big
loss, no doubt."

But it also turned out to be a great gain for the
Mariners. Davis homered in his second, fifth and seventeenth major league at-bats. Then, in his next nine at-bats
he hit four doubles. At the end of May, he led the
American League with a .344 average.

But Davis still wasn't convinced he belonged in the
major leagues. After the season's first month, Davis asked
Mariners' traveling secretary Lee Pelekoudas if it was
safe to rent an apartment. Pelekoudas thought Alvin was
joking. "I'm just fighting to stay on this team," Davis
said. "The job is still Ken Phelps's as far as I'm concerned.
If I get sent back down, I'll accept it and work harder."

Davis's hitting tear continued and he was named to

The sweet sight of a ball in flight   COURTESY SEATTLE MARINERS

the American League team for the All-Star game. At season's end, Davis had batted .284 with 27 homers and had set or equalled club records with 116 RBIs, 13 game-winning RBIs, 97 walks and two grand-slam homers.

Equally significant was the respect he earned among American League pitchers. Davis was walked intentionally 16 times to set a major league rookie mark. It all added up to the first major award for a Mariners' player when Davis was named American League Rookie of the

Year.

Davis became one of the first home-grown products to come up through the Mariners' minor league system and Seattle's first true baseball hero. In early May, after he hit a three-run homer to win another game, the Seattle fans cheered and cheered until he came out for a bow. It was only the second "curtain call" in Mariner history.

As Bill Plaschke wrote in *The Sporting News,* "This tradition-bound community, still treating the Mariners like new neighbors who don't mow their lawn, has thrown open its arms for a player named Alvin Davis. Those stories of a modest and innocent charm complemented by his ever-present smile, have made lukewarm locals finally think of a Mariner as their own."

That smile has been called baseball's best. And Davis's friendliness and sincerity back up the winning smile. Others may say it's his big, brown eyes that make him special. During that unforgettable rookie season, somebody in Seattle even wrote a song about those "Alvin Davis Eyes."

On his first trip to New York that year, the rookie was so intent on being polite to the media that he kept his roommate awake by talking to everyone who called. By June, his personal answers to every piece of fan mail were seriously denting his budget. Since he was only making the major leagues' minimum salary, he requested, "If it's not too much trouble, can you please ask them to send a self-addressed, stamped envelope?"

That was a few years ago, and now Davis plays for more than 20 times as much money. But Alvin Davis hasn't changed. He and his wife, Kim, decided during the hoopla of his rookie season that they liked their simple lifestyle and didn't want stardom to change it. They're still happily married and they haven't rushed out to buy things to keep up with the Joneses. At last report they were still driving their old Bronco — without a chauffeur. Reflecting a mature perspective on his success, Alvin compared his rookie season to the year any "Miss America" winner enjoys. "You have the pageantry and everything is exciting immediately afterwards," he says. "But then it's like being the reigning queen for a year. It just kind of dies down and things get back to normal."

After his rookie season, Davis's agent tussled for four months with Mariners' management over a new contract. Finally, it was Davis himself who came forward with the breakthrough counter-proposal. He signed shortly afterward. "It's unusual that a player would come forward like that," said general manager Hall Keller. Team president Chuck Armstrong spoke even more highly of Alvin's initiative: "I just can't tell you how impressed I am with Alvin Davis as a person."

For Davis, the contract stalemate was something he entrusted to God. "I hit my knees; Kim hit her knees with me," he said. After that, even though they had no contract, they had something even better. Peace.

Davis heard all the media questions dozens of times during his dramatic breakthrough into the major leagues: Was it a thrill to hit home runs in his first two major league games? Would he make the All-Star team? Would the so-called sophomore jinx affect him during his second season? (It didn't, but some leg injuries did.) The writers, however, ignored what Davis wanted to talk most about — his faith.

Picture this interview with a writer from a major newspaper. The writer goes through the usual battery of questions; Davis patiently answers them. The writer asks if there's anything else that hasn't been told in the many stories about Davis. Seeing his chance, Alvin doesn't hesitate: "Yes, if you want a direct quote," he says with an urgent look on his face, "I'd like to tell everybody that Jesus Christ died for their sins."

"At first it really bothered me," Davis said about the omissions of his favorite discussion topic. "Now I've adopted the attitude that any time I talk to someone, it's a witness. I can't control what people put in the paper, but my responsibility is to let the Lord shine through my life every day to all the people I deal with."

To the critic who says Davis's stats belong on the sports page and his faith belongs on the religion page, he answers: "My beliefs are the foundation of my life, the basis of my personality, the source of my confidence, and therefore, the cause of my success." In other words, baseball and his faith go together.

In one newspaper interview, Davis told the writer more about his faith: "It's the source of my inner qualities that I feel are necessary to play this game. The Christian life is consistency, and that helps me, because that is what baseball is all about. Consistency in performance and consistency in attitude. It's natural for a Christian to go out and give 100 percent, even when he doesn't feel like it."

The faith foundation which is so responsible for Al Davis's success can be traced back to his Christian upbringing. His mother's influence didn't begin when they became college roomies.

Alvin speaks of both his parents with great reverence and respect. His father modeled outstanding character and taught much by example. "My father was a great man," says Alvin. But at age 51, Mr. Davis died of a heart attack. "I was nine when he died. I missed him terribly, especially in high school."

The loss of his father partly explains the special relationship Alvin developed with his mother. With Dad gone, the boys and their mother realized they especially needed each other and pulled together. Alvin heard no lectures on religion, but he saw that his mother's faith was alive and that it worked in her life. "She's such a special person," says Alvin. "I think the number-one reason is simply that she has so much love. She demonstrated that love by how she raised me. She worked so hard to try to keep things together financially."

Mylie, Alvin's mother, is now an elementary school teacher's aide in Phoenix. "I knew someday Alvin would be great," she says. And she communicated that message to Alvin. With a parent who believed in him, it was easier for Alvin to believe in himself. Just before Alvin became a teenager, he attended a week-long series of meetings that led to a personal acceptance of Jesus Christ for the forgiveness of his sins. From there, Alvin found courage from God to resist the temptations of those teenage years.

"My faith was really alive and active," Alvin says of that period. "There were difficult things happening around me, but God kept me from getting into drugs or alcohol or anything. I was a good kid. I had a good understanding of right and wrong because of the way I was raised in the home. But you have to take a stand, too. My parents led the way."

The thing that makes Mylie and Alvin's relationship so special is that they're not just mother and son. They're the best of friends. She didn't even cramp his style during the Arizona State days. They talk a lot about many things and they have common interests, sports being one of the biggest. "She loves baseball more than I do," says Alvin. "She loves sports, *period.*"

As wonderful as it is to have a good friendship with a parent, that's how tragic it is to have a poor relationship. Yet, that's so often the way it is between teenagers and parents. Why? Alvin believes it's because "we don't have the bonds in society that we used to have. Young people spend so little time at home."

School activities, sports, clubs, even church activities keep students out of the home more than ever before. Gone are the days when the whole family needed to work together to keep the farm going. People live in cities. They drive cars that take them away from each other more often. Parents simply have fewer hours to develop relationships with their children. And sometimes parents are guilty of not taking advantage of what time they do have with their children. But time is something that Mylie Davis always had for her boys, and Alvin and his brothers always had time for her. According to Alvin, there is no substitute for it.

Alvin Davis says this to young people: "You can't control how your parents use their time, but you can exercise control over how you use yours. There are so many negative influences out there today. Parents can't monitor everything. Outside activities are meaningful, but you probably need more time at home, too. Take time to speak with your parents, your brothers and sisters. Just talk to them. Take on the responsibility. And don't be afraid to tell your parents you love them."

Just be sure to help them off the floor afterward.

Alvin takes seriously the Bible command to "Honor your father and your mother." He's proud to talk about his mother. He doesn't just admit that he loves her; he tells people openly. What a contrast to young people who don't even want to admit they *have* parents!

Alvin would question Christian young people who claim to be serious about obeying God but don't want to obey their parents. He believes God's will is clear: "Children, obey your parents in the Lord, for this is right" (Ephesians 6:1). He argues that you can't obey God and *not* obey your parents. And because God is sovereign, you can trust Him to work out His perfect will through them.

Maybe you're thinking: "Hey, man, you don't know *my* parents!" Alvin understands, yet says that God wants you to honor them nevertheless. When you do, two good things happen: One, God is glorified; and two, He promises you'll live a long life. That's right! Look it up. The fifth commandment, Exodus 20:12.

Mylie is no longer Alvin's roommate. He has a new roommate — his wife, Kim, of course. Kim was pursuing a career in counseling, but has given that up for now because baseball and counseling don't fit well together. Imagine her telling a client with suicidal tendencies: "Look, can you hold that until fall when the season's over?"

But anyone who has a professional athlete at home can still practice a good bit of counseling. Kim lives through the ups and downs and streaks and slumps of Alvin's baseball career and fully supports him in it. Alvin is thankful, and so are the Mariners and their fans. That good listening ear is perhaps most appreciated during difficult times. And for a professional athlete, that often means during times of injury.

An athlete makes his living by using his body, and when his body is not healthy, it's hard for him mentally as well as physically. During Alvin's rookie season a sharp grounder off the bat of the Yankees' Steve Kemp took a bad hop and struck Alvin in the nose. He collapsed on the field but remained conscious. "I didn't know how serious it was," he said, "but that's one example of how my trust in the Lord helped me. I was a little scared, but I wasn't afraid. It was the human type of scared: 'How is my face going to look? How long am I going to be out?' "

In one way, the injury turned out to be a great tribute to Alvin's popularity. The Mariners had to call a press conference in Seattle just to report that his condition was good. Later tests showed that the accident had affected his eyesight. To remedy the problem, he began wearing glasses when he bats. The glasses brought his eyesight back to normal so that when he batted it was American League pitchers who had the problems.

Some people think wearing glasses is uncool. Don't believe it. Wearing glasses is actually very cool. In fact, it's the *ultimate* in coolness, the new trend, the wave of the future. Soon, Little Leaguers in ballparks all over America will be wearing glasses like Alvin's when they bat. They're already begging their parents for glasses at Christmas. Everyone wants to have "Alvin Davis Eyes."

And university students will not allow the youngsters to outdo them. A new movement has begun among them as well. Yes, students all over this great land are begging their mothers to be their college roommates. Don't blow your chance! Students, start honoring your mother now, so when you go off to school, you can be the best fed *and* the most cool.

They stung at the time, but relief pitcher Todd Worrell is now glad for the rear-end reminders he got from his parents. Without such discipline, would his life have turned out so well?

3

TODD WORRELL

Thanks for the Spanks

Teenager Todd Worrell, Pony League shortstop, was taking some ground balls from his coach when one of them hit a clump on the ground and took a bad bounce to his right. Worrell slapped the ball with his hand, but couldn't keep it from bounding away from him. Todd's coach immediately called out, "Hey, always get your body in front of the ball."

Worrell got mad. "You come out here and field the ball!" he shouted. He kicked the dirt, fuming.

Standing nearby was Todd's father, who didn't like what he saw. So, later at home, they had what Todd calls "a little attitude adjustment time." That meant discipline. Todd had little to say in the matter. His father's motto was, "As long as you live under my roof and my authority, you are going to do what I say."

Does that sound cruel and unjust? After all, "authority" is among today's least-popular terms, ranking right down there with "police" and "prison."

But no, Todd Worrell's parents are not cruel or unjust. In fact, he thinks they're probably among the most loving parents ever. If they had not disciplined Todd during his youth, he might never have made the major leagues.

Through that experience back in Pony League, Todd's father taught him a big lesson. "He was trying to let me know that the manager deserved a lot more respect than I had shown him," says Todd. "Also that my off-the-cuff response was the wrong response. I shouldn't have popped off and said something back just to make myself look better in that situation."

Todd says there were other times like that when he was growing up. And through his parents' discipline, he learned to keep his cool — an important skill in the major leagues.

"As adults we have a certain way we act," says Todd, "and it's directly influenced by our training and the kind of examples we had when we were younger."

Todd's ability to respect authority showed clearly in the 1985 World Series, which matched his St. Louis Cardinals with the Kansas City Royals. Todd recorded a save in Game 1 and struck out six straight Royals in Game 5. But it was Game 6 that showed Worrell's strength of character.

Todd entered that fateful contest with his team holding a 3-2 edge in games and a 1-0 lead at the start of the ninth inning. Just three outs were needed for a World Series title. On a two-strike count, Jorge Orta hit a weak grounder to first baseman Jack Clark, and Worrell ran to cover the bag. TV replays clearly showed that he took Clark's throw and touched the bag before Orta, but umpire Don Denkinger blew the call.

St. Louis manager Whitey Herzog stormed out of the dugout, "spewing expletives that would continue for the better part of two days," according to *Sports Illustrated*. The Royals' Steve Balboni followed with a single and, after a passed ball, Dane Iorg blooped a hit that scored two runs.

*Fast relief: Todd's 98 m.p.h. fastball brought 36 saves and
1986 National League Rookie of the Year honors*
COURTESY ST. LOUIS CARDINALS

Game 6 had been lost, and with it the Cardinals'
poise. Game 7 brought an 11-0 defeat, partly because
the Redbirds were so red hot. Herzog became the first
manager to be ejected from a Series game in nine years
. . . Joaquin Andujar became the first player to get a
Series heave-ho in 15 years . . . John Tudor took out his
wrath on a metallic fan in the dugout and had to go to
the hospital with a sliced hand.

Worrell kept his cool, however, during both games. "You hate to have a World Series hang on one controversial play," he says, "but I think God used that situation not only in my life, but in thousands of others' lives, to show that there are more important things in life than the World Series. People have wanted to know why I didn't lose control. That was just one of those things that happen in the game of baseball. None of us is perfect, only God is perfect, and I know Don Denkinger wasn't trying to mess that call up."

Todd doesn't look down on those who did lose control of their emotions. He understands how easy that is to do. But such situations help him appreciate the value of discipline in his youth. "I guess it goes back to the way my parents brought me up," he says. Yes, parents do make a difference.

Childhood discipline also paid off big at the crossroads of Todd's career, midway through the '85 season. At the time, he was struggling along with a 3-10 record as a starter for the Cardinals' AAA farm club.

Todd's manager in Louisville, Jim Fregosi, knew that his 6'5" right-hander had a major league fastball (clocked later in the World Series at 98 m.p.h.). But what about Worrell's inconsistency? One day, Fregosi suggested that Todd try relief pitching. It would have been easy for the young hurler to say, "Hang it on your beak." After all, he'd been a *Sporting News* All-American in college, so why accept a "demotion" to the bullpen? But, no, Todd had a different response, one that would have made Ma and Pa very happy. "Sure, why not?" he said.

Flexibility and respect for authority were rewarded. A hard thrower who sometimes tired in a starting role, Todd was perfect for short relief. "As soon as I got out there (the bullpen), it was almost like a little light went on in my head," he recalls. In his next 17 appearances with Louisville, Todd won three games, saved 11 and posted a 1.19 earned run average.

The Cardinals called up Worrell near the end of the season which, of course, ended in that disappointing World Series. But Todd's skill had been shown clearly in just a few games with St. Louis, and he kept on showing it in 1986. Still considered a rookie in '86 because he'd seen so little action for the Cards in '85, Worrell smashed the all-time record for saves by a first-year player (the record was 23; he had 36) and was named National League Rookie of the Year. Of 24 first-place votes, he received 23.

Relief agrees with Worrell, even though it's a job as hairy as working the night shift at a local convenience store. No, there's nothing very comforting about coming into a game with bases loaded and no outs. But the St. Louis fastballer says his Christian faith helps him find the proper attitude for such duty.

"I want Jesus Christ to be my life," he says. "I don't want baseball to be my life and God just to be a part of it. That's one of the reasons why I can go out on the mound in pressure situations. It's directly related back to my faith in Christ, because I don't feel that my life is based on what I do in this game. Whether I win or lose, I play my game for God. I don't put pressure on myself to impress people."

Todd grew up in the megalopolis of Southern California and there, at the age of nine, he placed his faith in Christ following a Billy Graham telecast. It was a decision that pleased his father, Roland Worrell, a general contractor, and his mother, Donna, a homemaker.

"Real special" is the way Todd describes his family. He says, "I have an older sister and a younger brother, and both our parents showed us a lot of love." The love was expressed in many ways, but one was in the approach taken by Mr. Worrell toward sports. "From the time I was nine years old and in athletics," Todd says, "I can't remember one single time that my father ever . . . put the pressure on me to perform. Never that — just the praise and encouragement to keep going. I remember many times, after a game in which I wasn't satisfied with myself or we just plain stunk, my dad always brought out something that I'd done well."

But was there a little conflict now and then? Of course — this home wasn't heaven, even if it was near

Disneyland. "I always bumped heads with my parents regarding school," says the '86 Rookie of the Year. He freely admits he didn't study as hard as he should have.

Worrell talks while sitting in the Cardinals' locker room before a road game with Philadelphia. Five teammates are huddled nearby, loudly carrying on a card game. Undisturbed, Worrell mentions another area of conflict with his parents — church. Todd didn't always want to go; his parents wanted him to. He went.

For one reason or another, Todd required lots of discipline as a child. He was just that kind of a kid. "I went through a period where I got spanked probably once a day," he says. "I didn't enjoy going through it then, but now I'm glad. Discipline seems like a harsh word, but it's because parents love their kids that they discipline. It's hard for a young person to see that until he gets older.

"My parents always made it clear why I was getting disciplined, and after it was over, even though I had done something wrong, I never felt like I was rejected. There was always that reassurance — 'We love you and we don't think you're a bad person just because we spanked you.' "

Eventually, Todd learned to submit to authority — whether in the form of a parent, a teacher, a coach, an umpire or God Himself. But it didn't happen naturally. It took love and hard work by his parents.

"I'm amazed at a lot of things that parents let their kids get away with," says Todd. "They wonder later why their kids do whatever they want."

Worrell pauses to look over his shoulder and respond with a laugh to the ribbing of his card-playing teammates. They're saying this interview is going too long. Todd continues with his thoughts. "I would have to go back to what the Bible says in Ephesians 6 about being obedient to your parents. God has put them there for a purpose. For a young person, the will of God is very simple — the most important part is to obey your parents.

"I think that when kids understand how important it is to obey their parents . . . then they earn the extra freedom and respect from their parents."

Todd's parents were strict, he says, but they didn't smother him with restrictions. "They gave me my freedom to a certain extent — more and more freedom as I got older and they saw I was maturing."

When it was time to select a college, Todd chose a Christian school, Biola, in La Mirada, California. He enrolled with the idea of becoming a youth pastor, but his fastball drew swarms of scouts. Todd saw the chance to reach out to young people through a career in baseball. And he made it to the major leagues, of course, partly because of all his parents taught him about life.

It's a happy ending, yet the story continues. On November 17, 1986, Todd's wife, Jamie, gave birth to their first child, a boy named Joshua Todd. Hey, little Josh, get ready for a happy childhood in a loving home — but listen closely to your dad. He knows the value of a little spanking when it's attitude adjustment time.

Some harmful habits almost caused one of baseball's most versatile performers to squander his talent in the minors.

4

ANDY VAN SLYKE

Major Troubles in the Minor Leagues

Just how bad can things get when major league baseball players use drugs?

Pretty bad.

"But," you may ask, "don't these players use drugs on a limited, 'recreational' basis?" Interesting theory — sort of like the basketball phrase "no harm, no foul." Stories of individual players, however, reveal plenty of harm, plenty of foul.

Consider what the *New York Times* learned from Mark Liebl, convicted for selling drugs to four members of the 1983 Kansas City Royals. Liebl said that he was once at a party in a star pitcher's apartment, and a batboy for the Milwaukee Brewers also was present. Leibl objected to the idea of giving cocaine to the teenage batboy but claims that the pitcher said it was fine. The pitcher declined to comment on the incident, according to journalist

Murray Chass.

Consider the experience of Tim Raines in 1982. That season, Raines's coke fetish grew so strong that he told the *New York Times* he sometimes used the drug between innings in the clubhouse bathroom. "I hid it in little gram bottles that I kept in my [uniform] pocket." The habit even affected Raines's base stealing tactics — "Usually when I carried it in my pocket, I'd go in [slide] headfirst." John McHale, president of the Expos, told the *Times* that Raines "probably cost us six, eight, ten games doing things we couldn't believe he was doing . . . He'd be on first base, and he couldn't run; they picked him off. He couldn't find balls in the outfield."

Consider what All-Star first baseman Keith Hernandez told the court during the 1985 Pittsburgh trial of accused drug dealer Curtis Strong. Although Hernandez claimed he was never addicted, he explained his use of cocaine this way: "It's the drug itself . . . It's the devil on this earth. It has a strong emotional lure to it. It took me 2 ½ years after 1980 (when he began using it) to get off of it." The next day, Hernandez added these thoughts for sportswriters. "Cocaine is a dead-end street. If I can be an example for your kids as far as drugs are concerned, don't mess with the drug . . . My advice to anybody out there is to stay away from drugs."

Once upon a time, star players headed toward Cooperstown, the location of baseball's Hall of Fame; in more recent years they've headed toward drug and alcohol treatment centers. Many great talents have fallen for cocaine. Dave Parker, for one, told a Pittsburgh court that, during his years with the Pirates, he helped set up cocaine purchases for players on other teams and sometimes even arranged for Shelby Greer, a convicted drug dealer, to travel on the team plane.

What can be done about drug abuse in baseball? Maybe Commissioner Peter Ueberroth has a solution in the drug testing program he has instituted and in the fines and penalties he has decreed. But there's an outstanding major league outfielder named Andy Van Slyke who has ideas of his own about drinking, drugs and

Made it! Andy dusts off after a successful slide into third base
COURTESY ST. LOUIS CARDINALS

baseball. Van Slyke knows what he's talking about because he's been there.

"I was a kid in high school who got drafted by the St. Louis Cardinals as their first pick," says Andy, a native of New York state. "And if I wasn't cocky and arrogant before that, I certainly was after. I really thought I was something special and I made sure everybody knew it. I played the next year [1980] in Gastonia, and that's when things really started turning in my life. I was away from home for the first time, had money, had a car. It was a dry county [in North Carolina]; no bars. So if there was any partying going on, it was always back at the apartment. I started falling into [habits] that I wouldn't write home about. I started getting into some drugs and a lot of drinking. I smoked a lot of grass. Once in a while there was cocaine around.

"I was doing everything that I thought was OK because the world was saying, 'Have a good time. You're a bachelor. Go out and get it and don't worry about the consequences.' These things continued to grow in my life, and I'm sure they had a very big effect. I hit .330 the first half of the season at Gastonia, and I finished the year at .270, so you can see the drop. I started drinking before games. I wouldn't think twice about getting high before a game. Going out [to play] under those conditions was kind of crazy but . . . those things became prevalent in my life."

Known for his power hitting as well as running speed, Van Slyke advanced to St. Petersburg (Class A) for the 1981 season, but he took his bad habits with him. In St. Pete, he says, "things came to a boil" when he broke his elbow at the start of the season.

"I was really angry at God because I worked so hard that winter and was having a great spring. It was the first time in my life that I was reaching out to God, but it was in a negative way. It's a typical view. When things are going good you don't want to give credit where credit is due, but when things are bad, it's *How could You let this happen to me?*

"As that summer went on, I started searching. The girls weren't really satisfying me; they satisfied me only for a short time. When I saw the verse in the Bible that talks about 'the pleasures of sin for a season,' I thought, *One season in Gastonia; that's about how long it lasted.* The partying and the night life were becoming very distasteful. I started searching for things I could hold onto, because baseball in the minor leagues wasn't satisfying me and all these other things weren't satisfying me."

Even after bouncing back from his broken elbow, the young outfielder-first baseman hit a paltry .220 in 1981, and he had just one homer in 94 games. But all was not without purpose in St. Pete.

"I started going to a program called Baseball Chapel in St. Petersburg. Now when I was young and going to church, Jesus Christ was a name that was mentioned, but I didn't get *excited* about that name. But Dan Baker, the speaker at Baseball Chapel, was talking about *Jesus Christ!* I laughed my way out of that first chapel service and said to another player, 'Did you see this clown? You've got to be kidding.' We both laughed at the guy, but there was something about Dan Baker that made me go back later.

"As I kept going back to Baseball Chapel, I realized that this guy was talking about things I had never heard before. He kept talking about Jesus being real in his life and about making a personal commitment to Jesus. When I was growing up, I always thought that if I could do the things I was supposed to do, maybe everything would turn out all right after I died. But Dan started talking about promises God makes in the Bible, how 1 John 5:12 says, 'He who has the Son has the life; he who does not have the Son of God does not have the life.'

"As miserable as everything was that summer — I was just as miserable off the field as I was on — I decided I had to do something in my life to change. So after a game near the end of the season, when everybody had gone home, I went out to home plate at Al Lang Field and got down on my knees and said, 'Lord, I've had enough. I want You to take over my life because I can't do it any more, and I don't want to do it any more. I want You to come into my life, and I want to proclaim You as my Lord and Savior.' At the time, I didn't fully understand what I was doing, but I knew for the first time that I had eternal life."

But why pray at home plate, Andy? Was this another case of the Prodigal Son coming home? "I really think part of it was that I had been putting so much value in the game. I wanted to tell the Lord, 'I don't want baseball to destroy me. If I'm going to get to the big leagues and it's going to destroy me, I don't want it. The game is not that important. I want You to be first in my life. If baseball comes with it, that's fine.' "

Life soon became a little more saintly in St. Pete. "Some of those things [drugs and alcohol] continued for a time in my life," recalls Van Slyke, "but as I grew closer to the Lord, those things were not important in my life anymore. Drugs faded out, the partying with the alcohol faded out, the women faded out. I realized that the guilt was lifted. Forgiveness was given to me just like eternal life. I was living guilt-free for the first time."

Did Andy's new life without drugs, booze and guilt help release his talent? The stats say a loud "yes." Van Slyke went to the Arkansas Travelers (Class AA) for 1982 where he Van Smacked 16 home runs and Van Swiped 37 bases. His batting average rose to .290, an increase of 70 points in a higher league.

The next spring, at the Cardinals' Florida camp, Kevin Horrigan of the *St. Louis Post-Dispatch* saw Andy's potential. "If you liked Willie McGee," wrote Horrigan, "you're going to love Andy Van Slyke. It may take another year or two, but this kid looks like a player."

In 1983, Andy hit .368 for Louisville (AAA) before being promoted mid-year to St. Louis. Van Slyke's major league career has been marked by an ability to help his team in many ways. In 1985, for example, he helped the Cards capture the National League title with 34 stolen bases, 13 homers (second best on the team), and an errorless season in right field. Not only does the player known as "Slick" have power, speed, and a rifle arm, but he's versatile — Andy has played first base, third base, and all the outfield positions.

Andy's skills have always drawn the interest of many major league teams. Trade rumors were constant for several years, but they served only to bring out the special Van Slyke sense of humor. Told of a possible trade to San Diego in 1986, Andy said he'd rather stay in St. Louis. The reason? "My flowers just came up. My shrubbery looks good. My grass is really seeded well. To leave all that would be devastating."

But the subject of trade became a serious one on

April 1, 1987 (April Fool's Day!), when Andy and catcher Mike LaValliere were dealt to the Pittsburgh Pirates for four-time All-Star catcher Tony Pena. Despite all the trade talk of the past, Van Slyke was surprised.

"I thought I was pretty secure (in St. Louis), and it just goes to show that you can't put your security in anything in this world," said Andy. "At first I didn't know how to deal with it. It was a shock. But I think it's going to be a good, maturing time for me and my family. We've prayed and put all our questions onto the Lord. That's very comforting, something you can't understand unless you experience it — it's like a warm blanket around you."

Van Slyke has been careful not to neglect the spiritual life he discovered in St. Petersburg. He says he's enjoyed Christian fellowship with various teammates. "Who you're with is very, very important," he says. "The game of baseball is not the most important thing in my life, but I'll fall into [thinking] that many times during the summer." At those times, he says, talking with Christian teammates and reading the Bible help him regain his sights.

Most of all, Andy wants to keep his friendship with Christ in focus. "He's my Lord and He's my friend," he says. "What's a friend for? Someone you can go to, someone you can rely on, someone you're not afraid to say anything to. He's the greatest friend the world has ever had."

Van Slyke, known for his wit and grin, often talks to young people about his past involvement with drugs and drinking. "If it wasn't for the Lord intervening in my life," he'll often say, "I'm scared to think where I'd be today. Those things would have continued in my life and probably would have ruined me.

"I firmly believe that you can't succeed and take drugs at the same time. There's absolutely no way. I don't care who you are. Drugs take you down spiritually, mentally and physically. You can't concentrate. You doubt yourself because you're depending on something that is totally foreign to you. I always doubted myself — it was an escape."

And he wasn't the only one escaping in the minor leagues. "I was really kind of surprised at the number of individuals [using drugs and alcohol]," says Andy. "There wasn't that much cocaine, because it's expensive. But the alcohol and marijuana were enough to get anybody sick physically."

Andy comes from a strong, loving, all-American family (his father is a high school principal; his mother teaches religion). So why, with such a stable upbringing, was the young ballplayer vulnerable to drinking and drugs? He says it was because of a lack of spiritual strength. "I had no relationship with Christ to lean on, so I was leaning on the world and peer pressure. When my roommates were doing drugs, I fell into it. I looked up to them at the time."

Thus, based on his own experience, Andy tells others to seek Christ, not just to avoid drugs. "The problem goes beyond the marijuana or the beer. It goes within the heart. Someone who dies without the Lord is forever in damnation, whether he's taken drugs or not." The words are strong but there's no malice in Andy's voice. He cares enough to warn others.

What about the answer to drugs in baseball? Should drug tests be continued at both the minor and major leage levels? Seems reasonable. Should the commissioner continue to discipline drug users in baseball? Of course. But Andy Van Slyke believes the best solution is the one that's eternal. He'd like his fellow ballplayers, both those who use drugs and those who do not, to take a good, hard look at the person of Jesus Christ.

These days he's putting together some hefty stats as a big league hitter. But as a teenager, he almost added his name to the suicide records.

5

GLENN DAVIS

Almost a Statistic

People ask "Why?" when a teenager commits suicide. "Why would such a lovely girl take her life?" "Why would a boy with so much to live for decide to end it all?" "Why would four teenagers commit joint suicide in a car filled with carbon monoxide fumes?"

Glenn Davis doesn't ask "Why?" He certainly thinks teen suicide is tragic. He probably also thinks it's stupid. But he doesn't ask "Why?"

On many, many nights during his youth, Davis would sit in his bedroom, holding a .25-caliber automatic pistol. Sometimes the gun was loaded; sometimes not. "I would put a gun to my head with no bullets in the chamber and just sit there on the bed and pull the trigger over and over," recalls Davis, now an All-Star first baseman in the major leagues.

"I used to sit there and try to imagine what it would

look like. I would try to decide whether I wanted my brains to end up on this side of the room or that side.

"I knew that if I did that, it would hurt my mother and father, that they would be sorry for what they had done to me . . . "

* * *

It is an evening in late February, and Glenn Davis is casually munching popcorn in a Kissimmee, Florida, condominium near the Astros' spring training headquarters just a few miles down the road from Disney World. Glenn is the very picture of relaxation, but the story he begins to tell is far from relaxing. "I came from a busted family," says the native of Jacksonville, Florida. "I just didn't understand it. I didn't know why it was happening to me. The bitterness came from the quarrels between my mother and father."

After the divorce, caused partly by Mr. Davis's drinking problem, Glenn's mom tried to keep him from seeing his father. Perhaps she was trying to spite her ex-husband; perhaps she had other reasons. But as a result, Glenn would sneak away to see his dad and then suffer the consequences upon his return.

He was an unsettled boy in an unsettled home. His struggling mother tried her best to deal with him, but she was badly overmatched. When Glenn wasn't thinking about hurting himself, he was usually doing something to hurt others.

"I just had a wild streak in me when I was young," says Glenn. "My mother was a very strict individual and here I was wild and rampageous. Her trying to put a noose on me didn't work."

The young Davis and other neighborhood rowdies left their mark on the north side of Jacksonville. "We were into vandalism; we'd tear down anything we could. We were into robbery, breaking into people's homes, abusing other people's property to the max. We'd set the woods on fire, we'd set people's houses on fire . . . we did everything."

Davis carried the nickname of "Fat Boy," and the only reason he didn't carry a police record was that he and his buddies never got caught. Several of them did pay for their misdeeds, however. There was at least one incident of drowning in a pond where swimming was forbidden and at least one accidental shooting of a boy while he was playing with a gun.

Davis got such an early start on delinquency that many of his capers took place during elementary school years. During these same years, however, he also was forced by his mom to attend church. And that's where "the act" began.

"I knew what the pastor taught; I sat in all the services," says Glenn, between mouthfuls of popcorn. "I knew every word he was going to say. I just never got anything out of it . . . I don't know why. I guess the more I was forced to be in church, the more I didn't like it, and the more I began to have a cold, hardened heart. But I learned how the people in church acted, and I got the act down pretty well. I knew how to talk — how to tell them I was a Christian real quick so they would leave me alone.

"I thought a lot of this [Christianity] was sissy stuff — I just didn't want to be bothered with it. So, any time I got around Christian people I became the best Christian there ever was — 'Praise the Lord,' 'Hallelujah,' 'Thank You Lord this,' and 'Thank You Lord that.' "

The future Astro behaved a lot less religiously in school. Although he usually got A's and B's, his behavior gave evidence of home-bred hostility.

"I probably hold the record for getting expelled in the fifth grade," recalls Glenn. "Once I hit the principal between the eyes and busted his glasses. Every time I'd go to see him, he'd always tell me how many times he was going to spank me. But it would never bother me. The man would spank me as hard as he could, and I'd turn around and start laughing. But this particular day he told me that he was going to swat me three times and then he hit me a fourth time. So I just turned around and hit him as hard as I could."

Not much had changed by the seventh grade, except that each school administrator was probably warned to keep his guard up around Glenn Davis. "Every day or every other day I'd be sent down to the office to get whupped or counseled or whatever. I still hold the record for referrals [at Highlands Junior High School] — 57 times in one year."

Glenn would try to take out his unhappiness on others — "I even threatened to take kids' lives" — but there was always plenty of sorrow left within him. "The sadness came when I saw other children who had parents, and they would have such good times together." Always there was the idea of suicide — if Davis wasn't playing with a gun, he was holding a knife to his stomach. "I felt like an ugly duckling, unloved and alone in the world."

Eighth grade brought a new escape. Glenn had begun to attract attention for his athletic talents, and he thrived on the praise he got from his coaches. "The only people I respected were my coaches," he says, "and I really loved them. I was probably the most coachable person there ever could be. But when I got away from sports and back in my home atmosphere, I'd have to do something to get my frustrations out." Still, the self-identity Glenn found in sports led to a more mellow behavior — he was sent to the school office only once or twice that year.

The new image also carried over into church. "The people would acknowledge me for my progress and for the good things I had done. So I said to myself, *I really want to be accepted by these people.* Fearing that they wouldn't like him if they knew the real Glenn, he further developed "the act." "I became a movie star," says Davis, referring to the false role he played. "Every time I got around Christians, I wanted to fool 'em. I thought I had to fool 'em to be accepted."

But status with others didn't bring happiness. "I wanted to kill myself because I felt nobody cared for me or loved me. I guess what stopped me was baseball. I figured, 'Hey, if you're dead, you can't play the game.' "

Despite all the problems, Glenn's mother didn't give

up trying to raise her son properly. She tried discipline, seeking to instill obedience by striking him with a belt. And though she had to sacrifice financially, she decided to enroll the troubled boy in University Christian High School for tenth grade.

Did Glenn look forward to the spiritual enlightenment he would receive? Not a chance. "That stuff didn't faze me. I just found new friends there; I picked out the rowdy type of individual. A lot of them couldn't believe the stuff I'd do, but they started looking up to me and respecting me because I was from the north side of town. The north side had a lot of rednecks; the south side kids were, I guess, the spoiled kids."

Glenn scoops the final kernels of popcorn from the bowl. He tells about one of his classmates, another Davis boy — George Earl Davis, Jr., whom you'll meet later in this book by the name "Storm." "When I first got there," remembers Glenn, "I was kind of fighting against Storm. He was a good athlete and he was one of the key figures in the school. I wanted to prove I was better than him. I wanted to prove I was better than all of them . . . they were rich kids."

Although it took a while for Glenn to view Storm as a friend, there was no such delay in accepting Storm's dad. George Earl Davis, Sr., was the football and baseball coach at University Christian, and he showed a lot of interest in the new boy. "I listened to him, I trusted him, and I did what he wanted me to do," says Glenn. "I couldn't wait to get to school (each day) to see him, to say hello."

Glenn had brought plenty of athletic talent to University Christian (he and Storm eventually led the school to two state championships in baseball), but he also brought "the act." Except for when he was hanging around with the school's rowdier students, Glenn played the part of a "fine Christian boy." "I tell you, I had it down to the state of the art. I had it well-planned and well-memorized. I could have convinced anybody." Anybody, that is, who didn't observe his after-school activities.

In eleventh grade, Glenn broke his arm playing football, and the injury forced the insertion of a metal plate into his arm. He "turned to Christ" then, but in a manner that reflected his lack of a true faith. "My life was sports, and it was gone. I thought I'd never be able to play again. So I thought, *Maybe this Jesus who I'm hearing about all the time can come and help me. Maybe if I invite Him into my life, He'll heal my arm . . . and I can get back out on the field.* So when the pastor came [to the hospital], I said, 'Hey, Pastor, I don't know Jesus. Tell me about Him so I can make things right.' I prayed a prayer to Jesus and eventually my arm healed. Then I completely forgot about Him and went back to my old habits."

The old habits, however, were expanding into some new activities. "I started getting into other things — women, alcohol and drugs. This was what everybody was talking about, the thing to do. I found out the different thrills in the world."

When Glenn reached age 17, he realized a long-held ambition — he legally moved away from home. Asked by Coach Davis where he planned to live, Glenn answered, "I don't know." Said the coach, who just happened to have the same last name plus plenty of love, "We want you to come live with us. We want to invite you into our family."

That, says Glenn, is when he and Storm became close friends. "I lived there with their family [Mr. and Mrs. Davis, Storm and his sister, Ginger]. Mrs. Davis (Norma) started being a mother to me. They showed me what love was all about, what a family was all about.

"But I tried to fake them out, too. I started getting really interested in the pleasures of the world — the girls, the bar scene. I would play behind their backs so they wouldn't know it."

Glenn's wife, Teresa, comes into the room to replenish the popcorn; he continues his story. Following their senior year in high school, Storm was picked in the fourth round of the major league baseball draft, but Glenn wasn't selected until the twelfth. So Glenn enrolled at the University of Georgia, where he did some prodigious slugging and partying. Because of a coaching change at Georgia, he attended a junior college the next year and again hit the ball and hit the bars.

Major league scouts finally were sold on Davis's muscle, and he was drafted by the Astros in the first round of the January, 1981 draft, secondary phase. "I loved pro ball," says Glenn, "because I thought I had the world by the tail. I signed for a good bonus, something around $30,000 or $35,000. I had nice clothes. I had a nice, snazzy little condominium. I wanted people to accept me any way I could figure. I'd find it [acceptance] in the bars, the drinking, the party life in baseball. Then it started to dawn on me: *What is all this about?*

"I would sit in my room at nights and I would think about dying, and it would scare me. I started realizing that these things I was doing were wrong. But every time that thought would come, I'd get a knock on the door and my friends would say, 'Hey, let's go out and party.' It never failed. Someone always would come to distract me and take my mind off these things."

And so it was the same old Glenn Davis beginning to climb the minor league ladder toward Houston. Still hitting the baseball with a vengeance, still insecure, still partying, and still putting on an outward show of Christianity.

Glenn couldn't keep up "the act" forever. Something had to give, and it did. "What started it all," says Glenn, "was Baseball Chapel. There was a chapel leader in Daytona Beach [where Glenn played Class A ball] named Pastor Scruggs. I though I had him fooled that I was a fine Christian boy and all."

After pounding the ball at a .315 clip in Daytona, Glenn was sent up to AA at Columbus, Georgia, near the end of the year. After the season, he returned to Daytona to pick up his belongings and spent one ungodly night in a Daytona motel. And who should walk into the motel lobby that very evening but Pastor Scruggs?

"I was feeling good and here he came walking through the door," recalls Glenn. "I just about died. He hadn't known I was there, but he just came up to me and I said, 'How are you doing, Rev. Scruggs?' He started to open his heart to me. He said, 'I'm restless and I can't sleep at night, just thinking about things. There's all these guys here [with the Daytona ball club] who I've known as chapel leader. These guys come in here telling me what great Christians they are and how much they love the Lord. But they're the guys I see getting drunk, using God's name in vain. Some of them are even married and they're out chasing other women. I really feel burdened for these guys. It's breaking my heart.' "

Glenn instantly put on his most pious act: "Yeah, Rev. Scruggs, I know what you mean. I'm thinking the same thing. That really breaks my heart. God have mercy on those guys' souls."

But then, remembers Glenn, "The Spirit of God hit me like a ton of bricks, telling me, *Glenn, what makes you any different from those guys?* And for the first time in my life I faced reality. I was never a man to own up to anything. But for the first time, right there, I realized that I was a hypocrite. I did not know Jesus Christ as my personal Savior and I was on my way to hell."

The script had been ripped out of Glenn's hand. No more acting. But what to do now? Because Davis had a few days' free time before he was to report to a winter instructional league assignment, he drove home to Jacksonville. His desire was to talk to his adopted dad, Storm's father, but they could never arrange a time together.

Finally, on the last day of Glenn's stay in Jacksonville, Storm's mother approached him very soberly. "Glenn," she said, "we're tired of being your mother and father. We love you and we really care about you, but you've gone against our ways all these years. We know what you've been doing . . . you haven't fooled anybody. If you need a place to stay and a bed to sleep in, you can stay here, but we're not going to be a mother and father to you anymore."

Glenn broke down and cried, a radical act for a young man so proud of his macho image. "It seemed like every sin I'd done all those years was just flying by in my head," he says.

He told Mrs. Davis that he needed to find Christ's forgiveness. She offered to read him a booklet called the "Four Spiritual Laws," but he told her he already understood the message. He knew God loved him, and that Jesus Christ had died for his sins. But he had never really believed it. Until now. "I prayed my own words," says Glenn, "and for the first time ever, from the bottom of my heart, I asked Jesus Christ to come into my life and save me. Immediately there was a peace and joy like never before in my heart. I was free! I knew then that if I died I was on my way to heaven, and that this was the beginning of a whole new life for me."

It didn't take long for the young ballplayer to realize that he needed to tell his new, true story. "I started calling everybody I could think of on the phone. I'd tell them, 'Hey, I'm a real Christian now. I've been faking you out all these years, but now I'm a Christian; I'm a real child of God.' "

Only the unpopped kernels remain in the bottom of the popcorn bowl, but Glenn's conversation remains fresh. Even though the hour is late, the major league slugger is more than willing to tell how God has turned his life around. Yes, a lot of changes have occurred in his life since 1982, when he placed his faith in Jesus Christ.

He reports, for example, that a healing of attitudes toward his parents is underway. "I love my mother now, my real mother, and the Lord has worked things out in our lives and mended a lot of conflicts. It was tough at first, but the Lord was teaching me love and forgiveness. He loved me and forgave me . . . He wants me to do the same thing."

The Jacksonville native has experienced another family blessing in recent years. On February 4, 1984, he married Teresa. Born in Korea as the daughter of an American serviceman, Teresa also faced the difficulty of growing up in a broken home. When they first met in Columbus, Georgia, Glenn told her about how God had worked in his life, and she also established a personal faith in Christ. Today, the two are so close that Glenn's teammates refer to Teresa as "American Express" — he never leaves home without her.

The years since Glenn's conversion have brought baseball success as well as inner peace. He played just 100 games with Houston in 1985, but even in the dead air of the Astrodome, he hit 20 homers. It was a new rookie record for the Astros, breaking Joe Morgan's mark of 14. In 1986, Davis smashed 31 homers (he became the second Astro in history to hit 30; Morgan was the first) and he collected 101 runs-batted-in. He finished second to Mike Schmidt in voting for the National League's Most Valuable Player and led the Astros to the NL West title.

Even with the accomplishments of '86, which also included an All-Star berth, folks who know Davis expect the future to bring even greater feats. Astro batting coach Denis Menke sees unlimited potential. "I think he's capable of hitting 35 to 40 home runs and consistently driving in over 100 runs a year. In fact, I think he'll end up leading the league in RBIs for years to come."

Adopted brother Storm loves to talk about Glenn, taking pride in his spiritual and athletic success. "He's so strong," says Storm, who compares Glenn to two of his former Oriole teammates. "He reminds me a lot physically of Eddie [Murray] and Cal [Ripken], because they're incredibly strong and God gave it to them — not weightlifting. I hear guys (other major leaguers) talk about how strong Glenn is. Even if it's not a home run, he can hurt somebody in the infield when he hits the ball."

And how about your brother's spiritual life, Storm? "He is sold out for Christ. I was talking to Craig Reynolds and Terry Puhl (both of the Astros) at a Pro Athletes Outreach conference, and they were really impressed with Glenn's outlook. He wants to serve Christ and be in the center of God's will. Those aren't just words. That's a lifestyle. It really is."

It could have all ended in suicide, but fortunately, it didn't. And today, Glenn Davis would tell any troubled teenager to trust Jesus rather than give up on life. He wouldn't promise a major league career like his, but he would promise peace and joy.

*He was once afraid to kiss
her goodnight, but every-
thing turned out all right.*

6

BOBBY MEACHAM

First Love

It was a pressure situation, but the kind in which
a professional athlete likes to find himself. Clutch performers overcome fear. Future New York Yankee shortstop
Bobby Meacham was ready, having mentally replayed
this situation a thousand times.

He paused for a long, deep breath, and ignoring his
still-racing heart, he stepped up to take his stand. The
glaring stadium lights blinded much of what was around
him. A quick touch to the pant legs dried his moist
palms. He looked around to his third base coach who
always signals strategy in pressure situations. But the
third base coach wasn't there.

Not there? No, of course not. This wasn't a baseball
game. Meacham simply was standing on a front porch
in Boulder, Colorado. That infernal porch light that
blinded his eyes did, however, remind him of the lighting

in a few baseball stadiums. But Yankee Stadium was 3,000 miles away. The pressure he felt was because of the pretty young lady named Gari Breeze who was standing in front of him.

Sound a little less suspenseful than batting with the bases loaded in Game 7 of the World Series? Don't bet on it. You see, Bobby was planning to kiss Gari Breeze goodnight for the first time. He was determined. There would be no chickening-out or choking. No sir. Tonight was the night.

She stood there silhouetted by the porch light that some forgetful roommate had left on. ("Or did they do it on purpose?" Bobby asks, reflectively.)

Good. She's not even fumbling for her keys. Meacham saw his chance and knew what he had to do. He gently took her right hand with his left. So far, so good.

Timeout.

Sorry, but we have to interrupt this play-by-play for just a minute. But keep reading, because we'll be back after a word about who this Meacham character is and how he found himself on this front porch.

Bobby Meacham grew up in the Los Angeles area, and as soon as he was old enough to toddle out to the local ball park, sports became important to him. Raised in a good family, Meacham was later educated at Mater Dei High School. This Catholic schooling gave him the moral foundation that may have kept him from sinking into deeper trouble when the opportunity arose.

As a sophomore, Meacham got into the wrong group. And that group was into music — to the tune of lifting stereos out of cars. "My friend would sell them after we stole them," Bobby says. "I didn't personally sell them, and I never got caught. But it hit me: *Wow, this is really stupid; this is really bad.* That lasted for a very short time [about a month], and I thought, *I wouldn't want somebody stealing my stereo out of my car.*"

Bobby also had problems with religion in those days. And he didn't mind raising sticky questions at school. "We had a principal who insisted on teaching every student who went through that school," Bobby relates.

No, not a new hurler: Infielder Meacham shows fine form in uncorking his throw
COURTESY NEW YORK YANKEES

"I thought it was great, and I really respected him. So I went up to him and said, 'Father, is it true that you believe if you're not a Catholic, you don't get to go to heaven?' He hemmed and he hawed and he never really answered. I asked, 'What about my father? He's a Methodist.' "

Though he never read the Bible on his own, Meacham did wonder what the book was all about. Maybe it was just curiosity. But whatever the reason, when he arrived at San Diego State University to play college ball, he was open to the invitation of some teammates to attend Bible study. "I didn't go at first," Bobby says, "but I kind of watched the attitudes and actions of those players after that."

Among the factors that finally drew Meacham to the team's study was a tough-talking, tough-playing catcher named Roger Bleir. A forceful personality, if a bit obnoxious, Bleir was a team leader who would motivate you, even if he had to cuss you out to do it.

So how did Bleir get Meacham to a Bible study, of all things: At knifepoint? No, it was simply the miracle of watching Roger Bleir's life change.

"Roger had the 'potty-mouth'," remembers Bobby, "the dirty language and all this yelling and screaming. He was that type of guy — you always heard him." But then Bleir invited Jesus Christ into his life. "The changes weren't overnight, but he was definitely a different person."

Bleir and another player named Steve Esau became the key Christian leaders on the team. Through them, virtually every team member had the opportunity to hear how to know Christ personally. And when Meacham and the other team members witnessed the changes in Bleir's life they figured, "Hey, if Christ can change that guy, this *must* be for real."

Meacham attended the Bible study for about a year and a half and eventually made his own decision for Christ, though he's not sure exactly when. But he knew for sure that Christ had come into his life. There were no major problems and it wasn't any crisis that brought him to that point of decision. That would come later. For now, things were going pretty well, unless you think it's the pits to have a pretty girlfriend (not Gari — she comes later in the story), to be named collegiate All-American, and to be a probable future first-round pick in the major league draft. No, it was more the peaks, not the pits, that Meacham was experiencing. He was bumping heaven.

But those bumps soon turned to hard knocks. And that brings us back to the pretty girlfriend. After all, isn't that where most of your problems begin, fellas? Meacham had chosen to pass up a college all-star trip to the Orient and play summer ball in Boulder, Colorado, after his sophomore year because: (1) pro scouts reportedly were lurking there behind every bleacher, and (2) he wanted to be near his girlfriend who lived in the Boulder area.

So Meacham arrived and the pretty girlfriend began to reevaluate her feelings and commitment and wondered if, maybe . . . Ah, let's just come right out with it. She dumped him!

And it wasn't one of those ego-stroking dumps where the girl says she *really* thinks you're *really* a neat guy and wants to *really* still be friends ("*just* friends," of course); nor a heart-ripping rejection like "Get out of my life, Jack!" which can nevertheless be more quickly overcome because you *know* it's over and you can move her picture from desktop to dartboard.

No, this gal employed the cruelest of all rejections, the "slow torture method" that sucks the self-esteem right out of you and takes away all of your dignity and makes you feel lower than the sediment mud at the bottom of the Mariannas Trench. "Yeah, she kind of dogged me," Meacham laughs, though he didn't laugh then. "Every time I'd call her she'd be out with friends, or she'd say, 'I'm going to see a movie tonight.' "

At any rate, though the girlfriend never came out and said it, Meacham was a clever lad and eventually got the message that he need not further inquire. And to think that to come to Boulder he had turned down a free trip to Korea, Taiwan and Japan with a college all-star team!

But not all was bad in Boulder. First, a couple dozen pro scouts liked what they saw in Meacham. Second, there was a girl in the stands who felt the same way, although for different reasons.

Gari Breeze *knew* she was going to get to know this Bobby Meacham two years before she actually met him. "I had seen a picture of him before," Gari says, "with his girlfriend [i.e., the one who was always going to the movies]. *Wow, he's cute,* I thought, so I always said years ahead of ever meeting Bobby, 'I really think I'd like to date him someday.' "

Another interesting decision was made independent of meeting Bobby. "I planned my junior year to transfer to San Diego State," Gari says. "No reason at all. None. It wasn't my major. I knew nothing about the school. Some girlfriends and I planned to go to San Diego State, and we did. I met Bobby that summer before my junior year."

Once they did meet, the attraction between these two rivaled that which the pro scouts had for Bobby. And that was pretty intense. "I was scared," says Gari.

But not as scared as Bobby. He got butterflies when he saw her coming to the ballpark; fear gripped him whenever he called her. And that brings us back to the front porch.

Maybe you're wondering how a guy who can play shortstop for the New York Yankees organization, who has met the pressures of playing in the "Bronx Zoo," who has faced Boddicker, Clemens, Saberhagen — *how* can a guy like that be afraid to face pretty Gari Breeze at the front door? Well, first, this happened before Meacham was a Yankee, and second, who wouldn't be scared? You're standing there and you don't know if this girl wants to kiss you, or if she even had a decent time on the date, or if she thinks you're ugly or what. Well, Meacham did get his kiss that night, and floated back to his car like a ballplayer floats around the bases after hitting a game-winning home run.

Soon thereafter, Gari transferred to San Diego State and the relationship began to grow fast in every way. In every way, that is, except spiritually. Gari wasn't a true Christian and Bobby was having his own spiritual problems, as we'll soon see.

Bobby's game developed even more than the relationship. After he finished at San Diego State, the St. Louis Cardinals made him a first-round draft choice. But here we must venture back to hard times.

First, there was leaving Gari, this girl he had grown

to love. Second, there was the hotel in Gastonia, North Carolina. (Gastonia is where the Cards shipped him to play for their Class A team.) You've heard of a five-star hotel? This was a minus five. It was dirty, with broken-down facilities, green algae creeping up the walls and insects creeping down them. And were those bats Bobby thought he heard in his room at night? Maybe this is where Spielberg filmed the cave scenes for his movies.

Perhaps it just seemed that way for a guy who was far from home, who was lonely and missed his girlfriend, who was having a lousy year in baseball, and whose TV didn't work.

Looking back, Meacham knows he could have endured that short season in Gastonia with joy, if his spiritual life had been in order. Yes, on top of a .185 batting average Meacham was unnecessarily miserable and he knew why. During those hard months he tried to tuck Christ into a small corner of his life. The Holy Spirit who had come to live within him the moment he had received Christ was saying in no unclear terms, "I want to direct your life. That's My job."

Jesus wanted to be Lord. But Bobby wasn't ready yet.

What does it mean for a Christian to have Jesus as Lord? It means that Christ is number one in a person's life. It means the person chooses to obey what God says through the Bible. It means the person loves Jesus more than anything or anyone else.

Bobby knew there were things in his life more impor-tant to him than Christ. He didn't want to give them up. And *one* of them he knew he *couldn't* give up. Bobby was absolutely, totally, head-over-heels in love. *I love Gari more than God,* he thought. Then he rationalized, *I know she's not a Christian yet, but she's open . . . God understands.*

Somehow Gari was standing between him and God. He wasn't growing in his faith. God's Spirit was telling Bobby that he had too many distractions and Gari was a major-league distraction.

So how did Bobby respond to the conviction of the Holy Spirit? He ignored it.

With this spiritual struggle at its peak, Meacham headed back to California at season's end for his long-awaited reunion with Gari. He was totally unprepared for what — or who — he found.

Gari was a totally different person. During the months in which they were separated she had finally given her life to Christ, and unlike Bobby, she had *fully* surrendered to His Lordship. As happens with some new Christians, Gari's spiritual growth rocketed from the start. Now, suddenly, the roles were reversed. Bobby was the one who was holding things back spiritually.

At first, they ignored the problems that were beginning to drive them apart. Neither one of them wanted to let go. "I loved Bobby," Gari says, "and I was afraid God was going to say, 'He's not the man I have for you.' So I really did cling to that. I would not give it to God. I would say, 'Well, Lord, I know I'll give it to You sometime, but I'm just not ready yet.'

"So I held on to it until that weekend . . ." *That* weekend was when Gari finally decided to obey God's proddings. She told her girlfriend that she was giving the relationship to the Lord because it wasn't working. "I didn't sense that Bobby was on the same plane that I was spiritually," says Gari. "I knew that we weren't communicating spiritually. That Saturday things began to open up, at Disneyland, of all places . . ."

As they wandered through Disney's "Magic Kingdom" that night, their conversation wandered too. Then one exchange of small comments on a spiritual subject brought their differences quickly to the forefront. That happened as they were riding in one of the "Pirates of the Caribbean" boats.

Oh, gosh, Gari thought, *this is the time.* She sat silently for a few moments and then the tears started coming. Finally, between sobs, she tried to explain: "Bobby, I can't be your Lord. You have to find God for real for yourself. I can't be a go-between for you and Him."

"You're right," Bobby said. "We're going to have to break up."

While those words crushed her, they were also the

sweetest words she could have heard. They meant that Bobby, for the first time, was ready to make Christ Lord of his life. "I knew," she says, "it was the best thing for his life, whether I was in his life or not."

So the tears flowed, and neither the booming of the cannon, nor the flashes of the pirate battle, nor the stares of the tourists could stop them.

Bobby and Gari drove home late that night with hardly a word passing between them. Suddenly, Bobby pulled the car into a park. When they got out, he told Gari: "Sit down. I've got to talk to you." She sat. And he talked. Out came things that he had planned to never tell her because of the guilt he felt, and because he feared she would never trust him again. Nevertheless, the agonizing story of how he had betrayed her trust with another girl in North Carolina spilled out. The confession brought renewed surges of tears from both of them. But he *had* to tell her. Something — somebody? — simply would not allow this secret to exist any longer between them.

Gari's response was equally honest. Her wrenched heart felt the whole range of emotions. But she knew what she had to do. "At first I felt selfishly hurt," she says. "But then I looked at the pain coming from him, just this incredible pain." She also confessed some of her feelings to him. But above all, she forgave him. She refused to hold the guilt over his head like a club. It was a struggle, but understanding how much Christ had forgiven her made it possible. To do anything less would have been hypocritical.

Jesus wanted to be Lord of both their lives. He took away what they had clung to just as a father takes a dangerous object from his child. But He gave them something better in return — a relationship healed by forgiveness and built on trust.

Bobby and Gari were married, but it was certainly no easy stroll to the altar. And now, having married, the Meachams find they must work even harder to keep their lives and marriage Christ-centered. God has taught them a lot about relationships along the way, and they relate some of those lessons while they relax in the living room of their New Jersey apartment, just 10 minutes across the Hudson River from Yankee Stadium.

"I can tell any couple," Bobby says, "they won't be happy with the plan they have for their life if it's not the same as the Lord's plan." That, of course, includes boyfriend/girlfriend relationships. The Meachams had to be willing to give up that relationship if God had called them to do so before they were married.

"It's tough to give up what you think is right for you," Bobby admits. But Bobby and Gari strongly urge anyone who is feeling the nudge of God regarding a relationship: It pays to obey.

"Another key in a relationship is your motives," adds Gari. "When you really get down to it, is it to please God, or is it something that's fleshly?" By fleshly, she means a relationship based only on physical attraction.

Gari continues, "If you're committed to God and committed to being a disciple of Jesus, then you want to submit everything to Him, and that includes your relationship with a man or a woman." Gari talks while keeping an eye on Brooke, the Meachams' infant daughter. "I *know* that God was preparing me for Bobby when I was a little girl. If you really are intent on serving God then you don't need to be out trying to find the person who's right for you. He'll draw that person to you in a beautiful way and you'll know it. You don't have to go out and try to dig him up and ask, 'Is *this* the right one?' "

Bobby and Gari Meacham have no doubts about having found the "right one." Others would argue that there are various possibilities for "the right one," but these two, at least, complete each other in such a way that, well, God *must* have designed it. Gari is the more emotional of the two, more dramatic — a feature that shows delightfully in her machine-gun sentences.

"Bobby," she says, "was always very steady, and he still is. He's a very steadfast person. So God is teaching me to be more like Bobby, and I think I bring out more of the excitement and intensity in Bobby."

A lot of their closeness hinges on their spiritual relationship with each other and God. One of the most important ingredients is prayer. "When we pray together, it's great," says Bobby. "Usually she'll grab me and say, 'Let's pray about this.' The latest thing was about buying a house. We really needed to pray about that."

"You need to pray even in the little decisions," adds Gari. "God is concerned about them."

The two don't always pray together. "Sometimes I want it to be just me and God," Bobby says.

And Gari? "I feel the same. Plus, I think both Bobby and I fight against anything that becomes like a formula . . . anything that becomes like a stereotyped thing. If we both went to bed every night and felt like we had to pray together, we'd get into a routine and a rut."

For the Meachams, talking to God is only part of spiritual communication. He talks to them as well — through wise counselors, His Spirit, and especially through the Bible. And there's a third part to the spiritual communication process — talking to other people about God. That's not always easy. The Meachams find the hardest people to talk to about Christ are close family members and peers. Peers in Bobby's case means teammates. Are they open to the gospel? Do they laugh at it? Are they hard to approach?

"I'd say one of the hardest things is to talk with my teammates without turning them off," says Bobby. "Basically, I don't really care if they turn off to me, but I don't want them to be afraid of me in the sense that I'm trying to make them do something. I think I've reached the point where they know where I'm coming from, and I can go up to someone and say, 'Hey, c'mon and come to chapel. Why don't you just show up one time?' And they're free to say no, or maybe, or whatever.

"We have 10 or 12 people at chapel. You need that constant reinforcement from chapel leadership like Dave [Bratton, from Athletes in Action]." Bobby says that sometimes the non-Christian players will "razz" the Christians a little, but Bobby doesn't let it bother him. "I guess they're kidding," he says, "but they might as well be serious. 'Oh, we're going to hell,' they'll say. 'I'm gonna be on Satan's fire engine number one.' "

Meacham certainly looks down on no teammate. He's the first, in fact, to point out that *his* life isn't always the model that it should be. He even got kicked out of a ball game once, for laughing, of all things. Meacham was chuckling to himself over a call by umpire Joe Brinkman during a game against Baltimore. Brinkman said, "What are you laughing at?" Meacham said, "You." Bye, bye Bobby.

Meacham still loves to laugh, but he's a little more careful on the field. And recognizing and accepting his own failures? Well, that's part of life, too.

Bobby has overcome many pressure situations — the general pressure of playing shortstop for the New York Yankees, the specific pressure of a critical at-bat in the bottom of the ninth, the overall pressure of keeping one's job in the major leagues.

And kissing Gari goodnight? Well, that also comes a little easier now.

*These two Jays both faced
problems in youth, but they
learned how to fly over the
obstacles.*

7

JESSE BARFIELD
& LLOYD MOSEBY

Okay, Blue Jays!

$\mathbf{A}$ popsicle between innings. Chatter in the infield. Rubber cleats. Smashing little Jimmy's fastball over the 168-foot sign. Getting something to eat with Dad after the game.

Jesse Barfield enjoyed all these things while playing youth baseball during the early 1970s. All except the most important one — the last one.

For Jesse, there was no father to talk to after the game. His parents had separated when Jesse was a two-year-old in Joliet, Illinois. "I can remember playing a baseball game," he says, "and the dads would come and pick up their sons. Mom would pick me up, which was fine, but you'd miss going out with your dad, having some pizza, joking around with him . . ."

Jesse, now one of the major leagues' top outfielders, gives his mother lots of credit for the way she raised him. But, he says, there were still times of emptiness or confusion.

"I know for a fact that I didn't have the stability at home with just my mom raising me. I missed having a dad to go to, to express how I felt. Certain things, a guy can't ask his mom about . . . As a result, I kept a lot of things inside."

But why couldn't Jesse have spent time with his father, even if his parents were separated? Maybe he could have, but when Jesse was three, his dad took him for an outing one day and they were involved in a car accident. Jesse suffered a broken nose and a cut lip — and that put an end to their visits for a long time.

Ask the talented rightfielder to recall special moments with his father and you get a very brief report. "I spent some time with him during the summers when I was 12 and 13," says Jesse. "And then I've seen him in Chicago when we (Toronto Blue Jays) have played the White Sox. We're supposed to get together some time for a long chat . . ."

* * *

Lloyd Moseby, Barfield's centerfield neighbor in the Blue Jays' outfield, was raised in a tough section of Oakland, California. He had a father who was concerned for his welfare, but that didn't spare him from some shaky days while growing up.

"You had to be in a clique or you were nothing," says the multi-talented outfielder. "I was with the athletes. There was lots of swearing, smoking, having two or three girlfriends at a time. We listened to 'Earth, Wind and Fire' and wore high platform shoes."

Lloyd began his high school days at Oakland Tech, the school that produced major league star Rickey Henderson. Moseby's stay at Oakland Tech, however, almost produced a dead body — his own. Lloyd and some buddies cut school one day during ninth grade. Looking for some amusement, they went to a liquor store and stole some rum. So far, so bad — but the story gets even

(A) Reason to
smile: Jesse
has joy in his
heart and
league-leading
power in his
bat; (B) Lloyd
helps pace the
Blue Jays
with both
hitting power
and base-run-
ning speed

COURTESY
TORONTO
BLUE JAYS

worse. Lloyd wasn't actually much of a drinker, but this day he downed plenty of the hard stuff. And then he ran right into a moving car.

"When I woke up," says Lloyd, "I was in the gym [of the school] and my dad was there. We lived about 30 minutes from the school, so I know I was out for a while. I was ashamed in front of my parents and my friends."

The accident caused Lloyd to take things a little easier for a while, and so did his transfer to Oakland High School from Oakland Tech. But soon there was another rowdy peer group and other escapades.

Like what? "Like hurting girls' feelings," says Lloyd. "It was a game.

" 'Let's bet,' one guy would say. 'Can you get that chick interested in you?'

" 'Sure I can.'

"You'd date the girl for two weeks and then dump her. It was all a joke in the first place."

Finally, a young lady named Adrienne, now Lloyd's wife, put an end to the Oakland High dating game. Recalls Lloyd, "She said, 'No more!' And that's when I came back to reality . . . that this girl here, who never really gave me the time of day — no kisses, no intimacy — she didn't care about me being a big-shot athlete. She wanted me to be myself, which I could never be because it wasn't normal to be yourself. You couldn't be yourself, because it was uncool."

So Adrienne introduced reality to the man who would later be the second pick in baseball's June 1978 free-agent draft. And so did Mike Marcoulis, Lloyd's high school coach. He insisted that his players attend class and perform up to their academic potential. Today, Lloyd appreciates the coach's effort, especially when he realizes that some of his old buddies are illiterate. But he didn't always see things Marcoulis's way.

"I really resented him," Lloyd says about Marcoulis. "He used to take me to class by the hand, literally — he'd hold me by the wrist. But after I got into twelfth grade and saw how far he had brought me, I turned some of those people [his rowdier friends] away. He showed me that I didn't have to depend on somebody else, that they were going to hurt me. He told me, 'They're not really your friends if they want you to cut school and smoke marijuana. They want you to not have an education just like them. They want you to come down to their level.'

"Finally, I said, 'You're right.' And in twelfth grade I was diligent."

So had Lloyd Moseby won the battle of the negative peer group? Not quite. He was only 19 when he entered professional baseball, and he still had a tendency to run with the crowd. "I wasn't really a night owl," says Lloyd, "but I was just like one of the boys. My mom would always tell me that there was nothing out there for me but trouble. I was out goofing around, and I wasn't being the kind of person that I knew deep down inside I should be."

* * *

Jesse Barfield and Lloyd Moseby had something in common other than the fact that they both played outfield for Toronto and they were both born in the fall of 1959 (just seven days apart). As of 1982, both were afraid to be around Roy Lee Jackson, a pitcher for the Blue Jays who was later traded to San Diego.

It wasn't that Jackson slept with an M-16, had bad breath, or practiced kung fu in the shower. Actually, he was a good guy. But Jackson was, and is, a very committed Christian, and some people find that scary.

"At the time," says rightfielder Barfield, "I really didn't want to have anything to do with this guy. Roy Lee would try to talk to me, but I'd make excuses like 'I've got to go eat.' "

"Even though Roy Lee was a good friend," says centerfielder Moseby, "I didn't want him to get close to me."

Somehow, the righthanded hurler succeeded in getting Barfield and Moseby to join him and some other teammates for a Bible study in June of '82. No doubt the breakthrough had something to do with the fact that Barfield "figured I had to have a change quick — or else," and Moseby realized he was "lost . . . something deep down inside wasn't there."

Answers came for both men at the Bible study, as Jackson pointed out Scriptures such as Romans 10:9,10 — "that if you confess with your mouth Jesus as Lord, and believe in your heart that God raised Him from the dead, you shall be saved; for with the heart man believes, resulting in righteousness, and with the mouth he confesses, resulting in salvation."

That night Jesse believed and acted on that truth, and Lloyd renewed his faith in Christ with a determination to start living for Him. Jesse had found guidance that he'd lacked without a father. Lloyd had found guidance that he'd lacked because of negative peer pressure.

* * *

If you're looking for all-around stars in that cow pasture which baseball calls the outfield, Jesse Barfield would have to be somewhere on your list. His performance in the 1986 season provides one example of his varied talent. Jesse led all major leaguers in home runs with 40 and produced 108 runs-batted-in. Blessed with a gun of an arm, he led the American League in outfield assists (20) for the second straight year and won a Gold Glove.

Barfield's star potential began to emerge in 1985, the year he escaped platooning. Jesse is usually soft-spoken, but when he realized he finally would play full-time in 1985, his true feelings surfaced: "Platooning stinks."

"I love this organization," he said, "but it really hurt when I began reading stories that the reason I wasn't playing more was because I'm a streak hitter. I was hitting in streaks because they were only playing me in streaks. By only starting against left-handers, this meant that I was on the bench two-thirds of the time. No way can you stay sharp like that."

The Jays finally went to bat with Barfield's potential and traded away platoon-mate Dave Collins before the

'85 season. Said Jesse at the time, "I'm just grateful that now I'll finally be given a chance to repay that confidence. I promise you that if they give me those 550 or 600 at-bats this season, I'll fix it so no one will ever have to use words like 'potential' or 'platooner' or 'streak hitter' when describing me again."

They did, and he did. The Blue Jays put the bat into Jesse's hands 539 times, and he responded with a .289 average (up from previous years of .232, .246, .253 and .284) and became the first Blue Jay ever to combine 20 or more stolen bases (he had 22) with 20 or more homers (he had 27). He certainly served as a big reason for Toronto's whopping total of 99 wins in '85.

Promoting Barfield from platoon sergeant to field marshall helped release his potential — but so did that 1982 Bible study with Roy Lee Jackson.

"Thinking back on some of the things that happened to me," says the Illinois native, "if it wasn't for God . . . if it wasn't for me accepting Jesus as my Lord and Savior, I'd probably be out of this game or close to it by now. I had no peace at all. I was letting outside things get in, and when you're playing ball you have to concentrate on the things at hand. I was hurting bad."

At one point in 1982, Jesse recalls, he suffered an 0-27 streak at the plate because of distractions and worries. Tension between Jesse's mother and his fiancée, Marla, reigned as the main burden. That was one of the first situations he entrusted to God. And as the two women got to know each other better, they developed a "super" relationship. (Jesse and Marla were married July 9, 1982, and they now have two small children.)

Barfield, meanwhile, continued to grow in his faith, and his inner peace caused steadier play. "It [his Christian faith] has helped me become more of a solid ballplayer. I can handle pressure situations now." As an example, he cites a confrontation against one of the top relief pitchers in history. "The first time I faced Goose Gossage was in 1982 in Yankee Stadium. He struck me out on four pitches. I took one of them, and the other three were over my head but I swung. I was so intimidated by this guy — him being the Goose.

"After I became a born-again, Spirit-filled Christian, there was a fire inside me. I was different inside — I had that bulldog tenacity. The next time I faced Goose, I could hardly wait to get in that batter's box. I doubled off the wall to win the game. And then the next time I faced him after that, I hit a home run to win the game. I was just praying, 'God, give me the strength right now to do what needs to be done.' "

According to Moseby, Barfield is a big help in the Blue Jays' outfield. "If I didn't have Jesse," says Lloyd, "it would be a tough experience. Sometimes I'm out there, not having the best day, and he'll come over and share a Scripture verse about how I should be joyous."

Although Barfield's faith applies to his baseball career, he doesn't limit his life with Jesus to the locker room. He relates many aspects of life to spiritual principles.

Concerning racial tensions, for example, Jesse says, "We have to realize who the enemy is. The black man is blaming the white man. The white man is blaming the black man. But look at it this way. Can you imagine a bull in a bullfight if he knew that the red cape was not his enemy but the bullfighter? That bullfighter wouldn't have a chance.

"You see, we're charging red capes. We're blaming each other for our faults instead of finding out who the real enemy is. The Scripture I'm thinking about is Ephesians 6:10-12 [which he quotes from memory]: 'Finally, my brethren, be strong in the Lord, and in the power of His might. Put on the whole armour of God . . . For we wrestle not against flesh and blood, but against principalities, against powers, against the rulers of the darkness of this world, against spiritual wickedness in high places.'

"To get down to everyday living, we always tell people about Jesus, but we need to start telling them about the devil, too. We need to know how he operates."

And how does he operate, besides using racial conflict? Jesse points to sexual temptation as a major weapon of Satan. "The Bible says that if a man lusts after a woman in his heart, he has committed adultery. The heart and head are two different things. When a wrong thought comes to mind, don't meditate on it and let it get into your heart. If I catch myself looking at a woman and she looks better every time I look at her — wait a minute, that's not a thought from God. So what I do is stop, get my thoughts together, and pray for that woman."

If Jesse Barfield sounds like a serious person, he is. But that's only because he's found joy and meaning in his Christian life which he wants to protect. He knows that the more he honors God, the more God will bless him. "God isn't like Burger King," he says. "You can't have it your way."

As a result of Barfield's example, Blue Jay shortstop Tony Fernandez chose to receive Christ. "It was June 24, 1984," recalls Fernandez. "Jesse and I prayed in front of my locker in Boston. Jesse saw I was in need of spiritual help. Without Jesse's insisting — and he wasn't pushy — I don't know where I'd be as a person or a player."

One of Jesse's chief goals as a Christian is to develop a strong family. "There are a lot of families that are separated these days; there are a lot of them that have problems. But it's a plus to have a family — for the kids to have a dad there. The Bible tells the kids to 'honor thy father and mother,' and it tells the parents to 'bring up your children in the way of the Lord.' "

Jesse especially enjoys the bedtime and mealtime prayers of his children, and the opportunity to teach them the Bible. And the mutual faith that he and Marla share gives them confidence that their home will remain loving and stable. Says Jesse, "If we're established in the Word [the Bible] — which we are — and we put that Word in first place, when problems come, we'll be prepared for them, instead of blaming one another. I had a rough time growing up. My kids are not going to go through the things that I went through."

* * *

"I can honestly say it was the Lord who brought me

to that Bible study," says Lloyd Moseby as he talks about that fateful night with Roy Lee Jackson. "I was rebellious, real rebellious toward Christ, because I thought Christianity would take away from my fun. I knew I wouldn't be able to go to the clubs . . ."

After Moseby renewed his commitment to Christ at Jackson's Bible study, things began to change. Today, he says, his life has changed "totally," and you can tell he means it.

"Sometimes Jesse and I just sit around and say, 'Hey, isn't it a blessing that we're not caught up in this [the negative side of big league baseball]? Isn't it a blessing that we don't have to let 0-for-4 be a part of our attitude?' "

If ever there was a chance for Lloyd to test his ability to rise above the 0-for-4 blues, it was in 1985. Here's a potential superstar, who hit .315 in 1983 and .280 in 1984, struck with nagging injuries and slumps. It's mid-season, the Blue Jays are tearing up the league, and Moseby looks as out of place as a vegetarian in an all-you-can-eat steak house. How else can you put it when the team average is about .270 and languishing Lloyd is batting .240?

But Lloyd's thoughts, recorded in the midst of his difficulty, reveal a spiritual view. He said he hoped his teammates "would be able to see me even in my down times, that I'm still the same." He hoped that when they later experienced injuries or slumps they would think, "I want to be acting like Lloyd was when he was in his rut."

Said the centerfielder, "I'm hitting .240 but still smiling. I'm playing for Christ and still hustling." Moseby, the team's chapel leader, wanted others to see God's power at work in him during hard times.

Moseby's Christ-centered attitude also may have made possible his success at the end of the '85 season. He refused to give up, kept plugging, and finished the season with a very hot bat. He smashed five home runs in one stretch of five games, finishing with a more respectable average of .260 plus 37 stolen bases.

Like Jesse, Lloyd cares deeply about his family. He

and Adrienne have been married since 1981, and they have two youngsters. They're still little kids, but Lloyd knows that down the road there's a peer group waiting for them — good or bad — and he wants to prepare them now with a Christian foundation.

"I'm going to try to be the mirror for them. I'm going to let them look at my life and say, 'I want to be like that' or 'I don't want to be like that.' We'll go riding horses and do all those other things. But when we come back home they'll hear me say, 'Without the Lord Jesus Christ, I'm nothing.' "

The highly competitive Jim Gantner scrapped his way to the big leagues, but baseball success couldn't make him happy.

8

JIM GANTNER

Even Baseball Left a Void

At age seven, Jim Gantner knew what he wanted to do when he grew up. He wanted to be a major league baseball player.

Okay. But so do half the other kids who ever played sandlot ball. Why does a Gantner make it while the others don't?

God-given talent obviously plays an important role. But a lot of kids who have talent never make it to the high school level, much less college or pro. Many of them lack the determination it takes. They don't work hard enough. Others lose sight of their goal and allow other things to become more important. Those things might include a part-time job, a girlfriend, or just hanging around and partying with friends. Jimmy Gantner easily could have lost his childhood dream for all of these reasons, as we'll see.

Bouncing a ball off the side of his garage at age five, Gantner already imagined himself playing in the major leagues. With that rubber ball and wood garage he developed an elaborate game. Each bounce of the ball off the wall had its meaning — single, double, triple or home run. But if Jimmy made the right catch — sorry, you're out!

At age seven, he started playing organized youth baseball. Suddenly it was no longer a garage wall firing the balls at him, but a kid two or three years older who stood on a pitcher's mound. But it made little difference. Jimmy was still one of the best among his peers.

Growing up, his friends were always his baseball teammates. They would get up at 8 A.M. and play a game. Then, because it got so hot, they would wait until evening and play another game.

That was the main excitement in tiny Eden, Wisconsin, where Jimmy grew up. Eden, population 350, lies near Fond du Lac, which is not in the middle of nowhere but might be close. Milwaukee is an hour south. In Eden, small farms and a vegetable canning company are the main sources of livelihood. If you work hard, you might own your own farm some day or work your way to supervisor in the canning company like Jim's father did.

One of Jim's brothers got kicked off the high school basketball team and soon lost interest in school. He and Jim's other two brothers never finished high school. They went to work at the canning company and never had a chance to see how far they might have gone in baseball. But neither the "Future Farmers of America" nor the canning company ever had a chance with young Jim Gantner. He was determined to become a major league ballplayer.

As Jim began high school, it was still important for him to keep up with his peers, and that meant keeping up with them off the field as well. His buddies were athletes. They didn't do drugs and they didn't sit in a bar and drink to get drunk. Instead, they mostly drove around and drank beer on the weekends. It was just the thing to do.

Heads up: Jim's defense has made him part of the American League's top double-play combination in three different seasons

PHOTO: *LARRY STOUDT*

And what else was there to do in Eden, anyway? Jim sure didn't find much to do at church. Church activities took up an average of two hours a year, time enough for services on Christmas and Easter. But at least when the Gantners did go to church, they showed up in force. Besides Jim, there were sisters Judy, Shirley, Patty, Linda, and Lisa, and brothers Mike, Tommy, and Jerry. That's nine children, enough for parents Elmer and Erma Gantner to field their own baseball team.

But as Jim grew up, there were problems for the Gantners which he could not help but notice. Sometimes there was too little money and too many children. Jim's parents had health problems. His father suffered from arthritis; sometimes he couldn't even walk. Both parents were in the hospital at various times, once at the same time. That was the hardest, loneliest time Jim can remember. The children were left alone at home to look after themselves. The heaviest load fell to Jim's older sisters. It was impossible to keep up with the bills. Jim remembers trying to read the Bible during hard times like these, but he couldn't understand the family's King James Version.

Jim did work part-time packing peas, but never full-time — time that would have interfered with playing ball. He stayed in school so he could become a major league ballplayer.

Looking back, Jim sees the family difficulties in a positive light because they strengthened his character. "I think it helped me a lot," he says, "because I knew I had to work for something if I wanted it. It wasn't going to be given to me; I had to earn my way."

Jim speaks from a sofa in his beautiful home on a private lake outside Milwaukee. Sitting next to him is Sue, a local Eden girl, and now his wife. Their three-year-old son, Mark, one of three children, chases down a baseball that Dad rolls across the rug. A fire glows in the fireplace, supplying a homey warmth to a cold, damp day in autumn. On the wall are several photos of him wearing the blue and gold of the Milwaukee Brewers in World Series action.

Jim is Milwaukee's veteran second baseman, one of the premier performers at his position in the American League. He has a long-term contract. His dream is fulfilled. Life is good — but it didn't always seem that way.

There's only one thing worse than a life in which dreams don't come true. That's a life in which dreams come true but cannot be enjoyed. And that's the way it was for Jim and Sue at one time.

Gantner's climb to the top was relatively quick by pro baseball standards. After finishing high school he went on to college at the University of Wisconsin at Oshkosh and after just two years there he was drafted by the nearby Brewers. He spent a total of three and a half years in the minors. As a major leaguer, Gantner sports a .280 career batting average. He's a model of consistency who has hit safely in more than 70 percent of his games. He is a proven clutch performer — in 1984 he knocked in 43 percent of the runners who were in scoring position when he batted. In the field, he's led the American League in double plays three straight years.

Above all, it is Jim's gritty competitiveness that makes him a successful pro. The determination that got him to the majors in the first place is, according to Gantner, a key ingredient for anybody who wants to make it. "There are a lot of kids with great talent who never make it," says Jim. "They didn't want it badly enough. They figured, 'I'm talented, I'll make it no matter what.' It doesn't work that way.

"Once you get to high school, you've got your stars. Then you get to college and it's all high school stars. When you get out of college it's usually college stars who get drafted, so the competition is that much better. The ones who make it are the ones who work harder, the ones who are willing to sacrifice more of their time for baseball. I'm sure it's tougher now, because there are so many other things to do in high school."

Soon after achieving his dream of making the big leagues, Jim was puzzled. He couldn't understand why he wasn't happy. "I thought once I got to the big leagues and was making money, had a nice wife and a nice family, bought a nice car and a nice home — I thought I'd be the happiest guy in the world. But there was still something missing in my life. There's a void and you know it's there." Jim unconsciously was trying to fill that void with baseball.

Ballplayers spend a lot of time traveling and waiting. They endure about 120 days a year away from home, and that's a lot of time in lonely hotels. That's also a lot of time to sit around and play cards or sit in a bar for social drinks. Jim was usually around.

"When I was drinking," says Jim, "I'd get carried away. Two or three [drinks] would lead to eight or 10. You know how you socialize drinking; it was just a bunch of buddies drinking."

Don't get the wrong idea. This wasn't alcoholism; one could not say that drinking was taking over his life. No, baseball ruled Jim's life. But he knew now that baseball alone wasn't enough to make him happy.

"Baseball had been number one in my life, ever since I was a kid," Jim admits. "It was a kind of god. But I wasn't the happiest guy, so I knew that baseball couldn't be my life."

Neither Jim nor Sue had a personal faith to give their lives the foundation they needed. "I would have said I was a Christian," says Jim, "just because I believed in Christ." But Gantner learned that just intellectually believing in the existence of Jesus Christ wasn't enough. Even the devil does that.

It was a Brewer teammate of Gantner's who helped him understand the issue. The man was Sal Bando and the two of them were competing for playing time at third base (Gantner was later moved to second). Bando, an outstanding veteran, meant tough competition for Gantner, then a rookie. Gantner did some quick figuring: "Bando is a proven veteran; I'm a rookie. They've invested a lot of money in him." Conclusion? "I'm in trouble." He went to the front office and asked to be traded if he couldn't make the team.

But Gantner never got his trade, and he is eternally grateful. Bando, a Christian, used the workout time at the hot corner to not only unselfishly give Jim some infield pointers, but also to tell him how Christ had changed his life. He fielded Jim's questions and encouraged Jim to attend the team's Baseball Chapel services.

Jim eventually went to chapel, and it was during a meeting in Cleveland that he trusted Christ to forgive his sins and come into his life. That was the first step, but it was the only step for a long time. Jim told no one of his decision. Maybe you've heard of a "closet Christian." Well, that was Gantner. And his closet was "security-tight." No leaks.

"Yeah," he admits with a sheepish grin, "the first couple of years were kind of quiet."

"I like the way you word that," laughs Sue. "Quiet."

"I really felt that when I first asked Christ to come in," Jim explains, "that was it, that He'd turn me around. Some people change quickly, but I didn't. I was still hanging on to a lot of things I didn't want to give up."

Jim finally did tell Sal Bando about his decision for Christ, but it was no "tidings of great joy." It was more like, "Sal, look, nothing's happening in my life!" Bando explained that Jim needed to read the Bible and spend some time with other Christians to grow in his faith. Hmmmmmm. Risky. That could even mean admitting he was a Christian! Well, of course it would. It wasn't that Gantner was ashamed of his new faith. He just didn't know much about it.

Eventually, he began attending a few Bible studies. That wasn't easy, either. "I was afraid to go to Bible study because I didn't know anything," he says. "I was embarrassed. I thought, *What if somebody asks me a question?* "

Sue didn't make her own decision for Christ until two years later. That came during spring training through her participation in a Bible study led by Athletes in Action staff member Donna Sigfrids. Donna and her husband, Mike, work as a team full-time, serving as ministers to the Brewers and other Milwaukee athletes. Their presence in Milwaukee turned out to be a key factor for the Gantners' spiritual growth.

The relationship between the two married couples began slowly. Jim was skeptical when Mike began initiating contact with him. That's understandable, because professional athletes are constantly hounded by everyone from agents, to investors, to autograph-seeking fans, to every kind of promoter. Could Mike be trusted? And perhaps an even bigger question for Jim was, "Am I really ready to grow in my faith?"

"I liked Mike," says Jim, "but I was shy about spiritual things." Mike tried to get to know Jim, and eventually they played some racquetball together. "I know Mike sometimes thinks he's too low key. But if he had been a real aggressive personality, at that time I would have run the other way. You know, it might have been hard for me to sit down with a guy like Billy Graham or somebody that's really . . . well, you know . . ."

Gradually, Mike began to teach Jim more spiritual truth and involve him in the team Bible studies. But this process called "discipleship" doesn't just mean teaching positive things. It also means bringing out things in a Christian's life that are not right.

That became necessary when Mike heard Jim had been out drinking a couple of days after publicly declaring his faith in Christ. They met and talked at the Milwaukee Civic Arena, and Mike confronted Jim with the glaring difference between his public and private testimony.

Jim knew his drinking had gone too far and recognized the hypocrisy in his life. About his drinking bouts on the road, he says, "The next day you'd wake up and all day your conscience would tell you 'It's not right.' "

The reproof from Mike Sigfrids proved to be an important turning point. Gantner began drinking less and obeying God more. The same was true for Sue. And the more they obeyed God, the more of His joy they experienced. They believe the same is true for every Christian.

Does God sometimes take away one's desire to drink? "I believe He does," says Sue. "I don't have any desire to and I used to drink a lot."

Jim also has an entirely different perspective now: "As a Christian, I regard the body as Christ's home for the Spirit. It's His temple." And speaking from his own experience, he adds, "A high school student, especially if he's going out for sports, should just stay away from it."

This brings us to the question, "Why do most students drink anyway?" A lot of them drink because they're afraid not to. It starts with peer pressure. That's why Jim Gantner drank. "I wanted to be part of the group," he says. "I didn't really want to get drunk. I didn't say, 'I'm going out and getting smashed tonight.' The nights I ended up drunk were because I just wasn't strong enough to stop."

But after he stopped, he found not everyone was thrilled. One teammate came to him and said, "What's wrong with you? You don't go out any more." But Jim didn't let it bother him. "That made me feel kind of good," he says. "Until then, I hadn't even realized that I was changing."

Another teammate took things even more personally. Because Jim didn't drink or go to parties with him any more, the teammate thought Jim didn't like him. This guy began making little verbal jabs here and there. "He became like a thorn in the flesh to me," says Gantner. Eventually Jim got tired of it. But how does a Christian handle a guy like that? "I tried just to ignore him," says Jim, "but I knew that wasn't the right way to go about it. So finally, I just talked to him face to face and said, 'Look, I still like you, but my lifestyle has changed. I don't know if you don't like me any more, but I'm telling you right now, you're still a good friend of mine.' "

That straightforward talk pretty much solved the problem. "I think the main thing is to tell them where you're coming from," Jim concludes. "Then they can do what they want. I tell them, 'My life has changed, so you should know.' "

While these were two exceptions, most Brewer players saw the changes in a very positive light. Says Paul Molitor, "When I first came here, he [Gantner] was just beginning his walk as a Christian, and some of the guys who had known him were a little skeptical about the changes in his life. They were waiting for Jimmy to fall back into his old ways. But he has grown so much in the past few years that even guys who haven't made that commitment themselves look up to Jimmy. There's no question about there being a more gentleman-like character on our club. He carries himself as a Christian through good times and bad times."

Their growing commitment to Christ also did wonders for the Gantners' marriage. "With Christ being the head of the home," says Sue, "it's unreal the difference it makes. Because of baseball and the time we're apart you tend to grow separate. But as we started praying together, a binding took place between us."

With his personal life and his marriage in order, Gantner is having a greater impact for Christ through outreaches. He has shared his story with kids during baseball clinics organized by Mike Sigfrids. Sigfrids also encouraged him to become involved in ongoing ministry. Mike explains, "I said to him, 'I'd like to train you to have a ministry where you get involved with people's lives.' " Jim accepted the challenge and the two of them taught a six-week Bible study. During the study, Jim was able to counsel with one young student and eventually lead her to a personal faith in Christ.

That's perhaps where Gantner is strongest — talking to individuals one-on-one. With the help of Sigfrids, Jim has led a number of individuals to Christ, among them a carpet salesman, an auto mechanic, and one of his sisters. "I try to make 'Lord, give me an opportunity to share your gospel today' a daily prayer," he says.

When asked why he witnesses, Jim gives two primary reasons. First, he's commanded to by God in Bible verses like Matthew 28:18-20, also known as the "Great Commission." But second, he does it joyfully, not as an obligation, because of the great things Christ has done in his life. "Even before I knew it was God's will," he says, "I knew what He did for me and how He could help others."

Gantner also points out that Christians are responsible only to share their faith, not for the results of their sharing. "Christ has to prepare their hearts," according to Jim. "We just plant the seed. He's got to water it and make it grow and prepare the person to be willing to accept the seed. You can't force it on them."

There was a time when this fearless catcher couldn't cope with peer pressure.

9

LANCE PARRISH

Peers, Fears, and Beers

What does your mind picture when you think of the typical major league catcher? The stereotype says he's the tough guy behind the plate. Foul tips and 90-mile-per-hour fastballs bite into his body and he doesn't even feel them.

He fears nothing. He'll block home plate to keep any runner from scoring. Even if that runner is on loan from the Chicago Bears and is called "The Refrigerator." He could even be on loan from Santa Fe Railroad and be called a locomotive. It makes no difference.

Our stereotype of a catcher is built like a heavyweight boxer, has a three-day growth of beard and bad breath. Behind that mask, he's ugly. He's missing three front teeth. His face looks like he must have played goalie on the dart team.

The catcher has oddball behavior patterns. When batters at the plate aren't looking, he'll spit tobacco on their shoes. His knowledge is limited to the numbers of the four pitches he calls, and the names of all the hitters' mothers-in-law so he can taunt them when they come to the plate.

Got the picture of a catcher? Now throw it away. It doesn't describe Lance Parrish, one of the best backstops in the game. He's a gentleman, mild-mannered, and doesn't even chew tobacco, much less spit it on other people's shoes. Parrish is witty, as well. When asked for his reaction to catching a 1984 no-hitter by Jack Morris, he said, "You can't do better than a bear hug on national TV." No, Parrish isn't crusty — his good looks have caused many teenage girls to wish he was single.

Why do people put such unfair stereotypes on catchers, anyway? Is it because they wear masks? The truth is that a lot of nice people wear masks. People like "Zorro," the "Lone Ranger" and "Batman." Nobody criticized these masked heroes, so why do guys like Parrish have to overcome the feeling that all catchers are crude or crusty?

A couple of the stereotyped qualities, however, do fit Lance Parrish. He is very solidly built and has a boxer's nose, probably the result of home plate collisions. And he's tough, able to excel at baseball's most demanding position.

There's a lot of pain in playing behind the plate. It begins in the knees that are so often in a squat position, works its way into the back, where Parrish has often suffered, and even takes a certain mental toll on the head because of the concentration that is required.

"You usually have total control over what's going on in the game," explains Parrish. "You have to get signs from the dugout, be aware of who's hitting and his capabilities and weak spots, and be able to relay that to your pitcher. There are so many things that are involved with being a good catcher."

All that is hard, but still nothing compared to the balls that pepper the catcher's poor beat-up body, bruising him and jamming or breaking his fingers. And lastly, for

Tiger turned Philly: Powerful Parrish has made himself an
American League fixture in the All Star game
COURTESY DETROIT TIGERS

catchers who don't "mind their heads" there's always the
chance of getting the noggin clubbed by a baseball bat.

Parrish learned about pain early in his pro baseball
career. In one drill while in the minor leagues, he had
to block balls fired from a pitching machine — *without*
a glove. "Our manager used to put me in the batting
cage and set the machine so that it would throw balls
in the dirt," says Parrish. "He'd set it so that the ball
would either go to my right or to my left. There were

times when I would walk out of there with welts on my arms."

Despite the welts and bruises, Parrish is thankful for what he learned. "I'd probably have a hundred balls shot at me, and after a while I could pretty much keep them all at bay. It is a unique drill which not too many teams use, but the guy who had me doing it used to be a catcher in the big leagues. He probably saw a problem which he found correctable only in that particular way. It wasn't any fun, but believe me, it made me a much better catcher."

But the hard work didn't end even after Parrish's debut with the Tigers in September of 1977. For several years, he had to keep improving as a catcher to rid himself of a reputation for allowing too many passed balls. "When I came to Detroit [in 1979]," says Lance's former manager, Sparky Anderson, "I could tell he was a player who could have it all if he wanted it. And that's where 'if' becomes a mighty big word.

"I've seen other players with potential who didn't go anywhere. They didn't want it badly enough. Didn't sacrifice. It comes down to one word — dedication."

Lance showed the dedication and now enjoys the results. Behind the plate, he's a perennial Gold Glove winner, and as of 1986, he'd allowed the fewest stolen bases per games started of any active catcher over a 10-year period. And if anyone doubted his arm prior to the 1982 All-Star Game, they didn't afterwards — Parrish threw out three runners who were trying to steal.

At the plate, this multi-year All Star often produces 30 homers and 100 runs-batted-in during a season. Among his many hitting exploits is a homer that helped the Tigers beat San Diego in the deciding game of the 1984 World Series. It's not surprising that Anderson often voiced admiration. "Now he's a legitimate star," said Sparky several years ago, "the best catcher in the American League and one of the top two in baseball."

Lance Parrish may be tough, but that doesn't mean he's never been afraid. At times he feared what other people would think. And because of that fear and his desire to be accepted by others, he let them tell him what to do. He gave in to peer pressure.

Like Jim Gantner, the peer pressure faced by Parrish also involved drinking. At first he thought it was kind of funny. But later it became anything but funny as it began to take his life down the wrong path. It took someone not so tough to turn him around, namely a woman.

Parrish tells the story: "It started when I graduated from high school and entered professional baseball. I was an 18-year-old kid away from home for the first time. I was playing with college guys; guys who had been in pro baseball for a while. It was a totally different atmosphere for me."

And not a totally healthy one, Parrish learned. "To be 'one of the guys,' the thing to do after the ballgame was sit around and have a few beers . . ."

When Parrish thinks back on his first drinking experience, he remembers that it wasn't much fun. Nevertheless he can't resist a chuckle over it. He was as much a rookie drinker as he was a rookie ballplayer. "I never had any type of drink when I was in high school," he explains. "So everybody said, 'Let's go and have a few beers,' and I said, 'OK.' So I go out and drink three-fourths of a beer and I couldn't even see straight. Everybody was looking at me like, 'What's wrong with this guy?' I felt like I was in another time zone. When I got back to my room, I just said, 'Oh my gosh, what's going on? What am I going to do about this?' "

He did nothing about it. Lance was afraid to say no. So the next time the older players invited him to go out drinking, he acted as excited as the guys in the Lite Beer commercials: "Sure fellas! What's it going to be tonight — Big Daddy's or the Elbow Room?"

"Stupid me," Parrish now laments, "I went ahead and kept doing it and kept doing it, until finally I could handle more and more and more . . . You just keep trying to push yourself and push yourself to fit in and be one of the guys. I really believe that's where a lot of drinking problems start and it's very hard to get ahold of."

In his years in professional baseball Parrish has seen a number of players whose drinking got ahold of them. "Especially through my minor league career, it seemed like after every game they would sit around the clubhouse and drink beer. After the clubhouse closed they'd head straight to the bar. This would go on day after day, and to be a pro athlete you just can't do those things."

Nor to be an insurance salesman, for that matter. Or a construction worker. Or a high school student. No one can handle that kind of drinking forever. "Sooner or later it's gonna catch up to you," says Parrish. "It always does."

Parrish might easily have continued down that same trail had he not met two important people. First, he fell in love with a special girl named Arlyne. And because of the quality of her life as a Christian, she helped lead Lance to the second person, Jesus Christ.

As it has been for so many other players, it was through a Baseball Chapel service that Lance committed his life to Christ. After his third or fourth service he went alone to his hotel room and opened his heart to Christ in this prayer: "Lord, I know You're listening to me. I believe in You and I want to become a Christian. I want to follow Your Word; I want to dedicate myself to You and live my life the way You would like me to live my life."

"I didn't say it quietly," remembers Lance, smiling. "I said it out loud like someone was listening to me there in my hotel room."

Until he told Arlyne about his hotel-room prayer, she did not even know that he had started attending Baseball Chapel meetings. She was the happiest person to hear about his decision for Christ. Also the most shocked. Up until then, Lance had not exactly been the most religious guy on the block.

Christ began to change Lance's life as he continued to attend chapel ("Baseball Chapel is an opportuinty for me to get to know Jesus Christ in a more personal way," says Lance.) It slowly became more important to the catcher to please God and the woman he loved than those who wanted him to go out drinking. Above all, he credits Arlyne with helping him overcome the battle with peer pressure. "It was like she was brought to me for a purpose," says Lance, "and the purpose was to settle me down, bring me back to reality, and put things into perspective. She's had an unbelievable effect on my life.

"I wanted to make a change for her," he continues, talking about the woman who became his wife. "I loved her so much that I was willing to do anything to make her happy. I was willing to put drink behind me. I don't drink any more, period. After a game [on the road] I go and grab something to eat and go up to my room and that's it. It's like I woke up one day and said, 'This is it.' " Lance and Arlyne now have three children, David, Matthew and Ashley Lynn, and all of them are proud of their dad and the role model he has become in the major leagues.

Lance Parrish made the break with peer pressure. He quit allowing other people to overly-influence him. Love helped him overcome his fear of displeasing others. But such a breakthrough is not easy against the difficult enemy called "peer pressure." Says Lance, "There comes a time when outside influences and people you grow up with are going to sway you in one direction or another, very possibly a direction that you don't want to go."

But Parrish doesn't believe in just rolling along with the tide. "Be your own person and take your stand," he says. "Decide what your principles in life are, which direction you want to see your life going, and then stand by it. People won't dislike you because you decide to take your stand on things you believe in."

Using examples he's seen in his own life, Parrish continues. "I've come across a lot of people in baseball whom I know others have tried to pressure into doing one thing, but they've done the other thing because that's what they believed in. It's fun to see that. You can see that guy's a strong person. I respect a guy who takes a stand and is his own person more than anybody else."

A special problem that most Christians face is avoiding negative peer pressure without distancing themselves from their friends. Parrish eats, drinks, sleeps, practices, plays and travels amidst his 25-man peer group for seven months each year. How does he handle this tension? "You can be friendly with anybody," Parrish points out. "I go out with guys on our club; it's just that I don't care to sit down and drink with them. I have a Coke or Sprite or something when they have their beers. It'd be very easy for me to sit down and have a beer or two with them, but I choose not to. I have decided not to do it and I'm not doing it."

Lance Parrish has won the battle with peer pressure. He's free to please those who really matter in his life — God, above all, and his wife and family. You won't see Lance Parrish trying to win people's friendship by compromising to please them. He's his own man. God's man.

Only by focusing on God could Storm Davis escape the distractions and fears that hurt his pitching.

10

STORM DAVIS

In the Eye of the Storm

You can plan for success, prepare for success, even dress for success, but there's no guarantee that you'll ace that test or land that job. Failure, however, is not so tricky to achieve. The following time-tested strategies are absolutely guaranteed to bring failure:
- Doing crossword puzzles while taking the Scholastic Aptitude Test.
- Discussing your last UFO sighting with a state trooper who has pulled you over.
- Talking about an ex-girlfriend or ex-boyfriend during your honeymoon.
- Thinking about anything except brains while doing brain surgery.

Yes, unless you're a failure fan, you'd better keep your mind on the job at hand. Success demands concentration — no room for worries and distractions, just concentration.

Storm Davis, now a San Diego Padre, learned that lesson the hard way while pitching for the Baltimore Orioles in 1985. Things got to Storm mentally in '85. Things like his 19-year-old sister leaving home; his wife nearly suffering a miscarriage; his contract status; fans and press hassling him for failing to pitch like Jim Palmer. Those things destroyed his concentration.

As Storm will tell you, you want to pay attention to what you're doing on the pitcher's mound. He still remembers, for example, what happened during a game against Toronto in April, 1985. The Blue Jays, you'll recall, flew to the American League East title that year with hitters like Lloyd Moseby, George Bell and Jesse Barfield.

Man, why didn't I sign that [two-year] contract? Davis recalls thinking as he faced the Jays. *How come my sister left home? I hope Angie [Storm's wife] is OK . . .*

The result was predictable, and Storm even provides the sound effects from memory. "Bam! Here I am not thinking about what I'm doing, up against one of the better major league teams, and I'm just getting killed out there. I got bombarded for six runs in the second inning and was taken out."

And that's the way things went throughout a stormy season. Although he'd hoped this would be his first season as a 20-game winner, Davis instead woke up in August to a 5-7 won-loss record and an earned run average well above 5.0. Even more startling was his ERA in the first two innings of all his starts: a whopping 9.09. He usually concentrated in later innings — after a few line drives got his attention — but the early innings were often spent in a fog.

Davis's performance was a mystery to everyone in Birdland, for no one ever doubted his talent. The 6'4" righthander was always compared to former Oriole great Jim Palmer — both in skills and appearance — ever since he joined the Orioles in 1982. After beginning his career as the American League's youngest player (age 20), Storm posted a 35-20 record over his first three seasons. He started and won game four of the Orioles' five-game

Bullet on the way: Storm seeks to combine outstanding fastball with restored concentration
PHOTO: JERRY WACHTER

World Series victory over Philadelphia in 1983. Although his first name has nothing to do with the weather (his mother read a novel before his birth in which the hero's name was Dr. Storm Linders), his 91-mile-per-hour fastball has blown away lots of batters.

Success, however, was out of reach in 1985 for both Storm and the entire Oriole pitching staff. The Bird pitchers stumbled to a disappointing 4.39 team ERA, the highest in Oriole history, and no one was any more disappointed than Davis. Why couldn't Storm put aside his personal struggles when he took the mound? Why was it that family problems produced home-run balls?

"The things off the field . . . the situation with my sister and with Angie's pregnancy . . . they might not have seemed too big to other people, but they were to me," says Storm. Why did the disappearance of his sister, Ginger, bother him so much? Because he loves her . . . because the family didn't even know where she was for many months . . . because the Davis family had never faced such a major problem before. And why did Angie's troubled pregnancy cause so much worry for her hard-throwing husband? Because they'd wanted children for several years and had been unable to conceive . . . because Angie almost lost the baby several times . . . because she was taking hormone shots each week to prevent a miscarriage.

Storm admits he could have handled these situations better. Other pros have done their jobs despite personal problems, and Storm had extra strength available from his relationship with Christ. Yes, he knew he should have handled things better — and that very fact sent him still lower.

"I felt that I was weak in letting things get to me mentally. What bothered me the most was here I was a Christian, had been around men and ladies who had weathered things like this, had the wisdom they had taught me and yet I was failing in giving things over to the Lord. It was really frustrating to me that I knew better."

A bundle of joy came to Storm and Angie on June 26, 1985, when Zachary Storm Davis was born. But even little Zach's arrival did not remove the pressure Dad was feeling.

The overall failure of the Oriole pitching staff (Mike Flanagan called it a "staff infection") brought out the boo birds in the bleachers and fears within each hurler. "Losing is contagious," said Scott McGregor, a normally reliable performer who ended the year with a 4.81 ERA. "When it was time to reach down inside, I think we just got scared. You can't be afraid to lose."

Storm agrees. "It was like we all had a phobia. To guys who've never lost, the fear of failure is so great.

Mentally, I was being destroyed by game after game of sub-par performances and the pressure of the press . . . of being hailed as perhaps the next Jim Palmer and not producing."

But Storm's real problem, he realized one night in Seattle, was that he really wasn't depending on the Lord. Storm had fallen asleep in his hotel room after a night game with the Mariners, but he was awakened by a phone call from a close friend named Dave Krueger. Dave was in the Seattle area for a family reunion and wanted to offer his friend some encouragement. The call caused Storm to reflect on a Baseball Chapel message given earlier that year by Krueger.

"He talked about three types of responses to Jesus Christ in New Testament times and today," says Storm of Krueger's chapel talk. "There are the curious — those who are lost but following Christ out of curiosity. Then there are the convinced — yes, they accepted Christ as their Savior but they're content to just stand in the corner and watch things happen. The third type was what God wanted me to be — committed — one who is willing to go for broke and say, 'I'm going to let You have my whole life; I'm going to start living by faith.' "

The Lord had gotten Storm's attention. "God kept me awake until about 3 A.M., dealing with me about these things. I wept; I wept openly. There was a lot of frustration and a lot of fear, plain old fear. I was not observing the old saying, 'Let go and let God.' I would not let go and say, 'Okay, God, they're Yours — the people are Yours, my life is Yours, my career is Yours."

Looking back, the Jacksonville, Florida native believes he may have had a tendency to take God for granted. "I grew up in a church, accepted Christ early in life, went to a Christian high school," he says. "I'd never struggled in baseball, I'd never had a problem with my family, and I'd certainly never faced the responsibility of being a father. God used these things to bring me to my knees, literally, in Seattle."

That time on his knees had a profound effect when Davis stood on American League pitching mounds. "The next day," says Storm, "I sensed a peace. The Bible talks about the 'peace that passes all understanding.' God had rejuvenated my love for the game, and things began to take off."

Storm won his next four starts, and showed his old confidence and concentration. "The way Storm Davis is pitching," wrote Robert Fachet of the *Washington Post,* "the Orioles wish they had fingerprinted the imposter who wore No. 34 in June and July." A line drive by New York's Mike Pagliarulo damaged Storm's right wrist and cost him several September starts, but he still ended his hardest season with a respectable 10-8 record.

And so, with the lessons of 1985 behind him, '86 must have been a great year for Storm Davis? Well, not quite. Yes, the powerful righty did much better in concentrating on the mound — he lowered his ERA from 4.53 in '85 to 3.62. But the Orioles failed to support him with either glove or bat, and he finished with a 9-12 season.

Storm deserved to win more than nine games, but he still lacked consistency in '86. And once again, a September injury cut his season short. This time, while covering first on a grounder, Storm hit the bag awkwardly and tore ligaments in his ankle. That play turned out to be his last in an Oriole uniform. San Diego traded two good players to Baltimore for Davis — veteran catcher Terry Kennedy and minor league pitcher Mark Williamson, considered a top prospect. Could it be that Storm Davis will finally become the next Jim Palmer — but in San Diego rather than Baltimore?

* * *

Although Storm Davis had known Angie Gay since their early childhood (through Jacksonville's First Baptist Church), he first sensed an attraction for her as a result of a classroom friendship. "I remember this biology class we had in our sophomore year," he says. "Angie would do my lab drawings while I'd cut up the little animals."

No, it wasn't love at first lab, but it was a start. Before long, Storm and his football center (Storm was the quar-

terback) dropped in on Angie and a friend just to talk.
Alas, the center had recently broken up with Angie for
the second time. Angie tells the story: "Here I am,
throwing sarcastic remarks at the other guy — a very
immature way to handle it. This other guy and I are
picking at each other and Storm's sitting there making
goo-goo eyes at me. I thought, *Oh no, I don't want this.*
So the next day, I gave him a note which told him to
take a hike."

But Storm took only a short hike as Angie soon
changed her mind. The two dated for more than a year
before Storm got his driver's license, so they spent a lot
of time together at school events, walking on the beach,
visiting each other's homes — mostly just talking.

"We never got really serious because we knew that
we were still kids," says Storm. "We remained on the
friendship level . . . we never went to a fancy restaurant
or anything like that." Today, the Davises are grateful
for all the time they spent in quiet conversation, getting
to know each other. Without really realizing it, they were
building a foundation for a successful marriage.

Storm and Angie have strong feelings about the do's
and don'ts of dating, and their happy marriage gives
others reason to listen. "We would start our dates off
with prayer and end our dates with prayer," says Storm
in relating Tip Number One.

"Don't date a non-believer," Angie tells teenage Christians in Tip Number Two. She supports that suggestion
by noting the Bible's command that a believer not marry
a non-believer (2 Corinthians 6:14-18). Because strong
emotions can get involved during the dating process,
she feels that the way to avoid marrying a non-believer
is to date only fellow believers. "You're going to marry
someone you date," she says.

And speaking of being careful about who to date,
Angie mentions Tip Number Three, which she learned
at Bill Gothard's Institute in Basic Youth Conflicts. "If a
guy wanted to date me, he had to ask my father," she
says. Although Angie had no choice in the matter — it
was her father's policy — she says she loved the idea.

"I really felt that if a guy wanted to date me bad enough he wouldn't be afraid to ask my dad. And it was one way of avoiding some of the not-so-good guys who wanted to go out. I would tell Dad, 'No, Dad,' and he would tell them for me."

Storm and Angie maintained a wholesome relationship that allowed them to effectively prepare for marriage. Wholesome, yes — but not perfect. At least not where a guy named Charlie Pierce was concerned. Poor Charlie. Even to this day, he probably doesn't know about the dirty deed Storm did to him just because they happened to like the same girl.

It seems that flowers were always sold at University Christian High School on Valentine's Day, and Charlie shelled out five dollars to buy some for Angie. "I saw Charlie," recalls Storm, "and I knew he had bought the flowers for Angie. I saw him put them in her locker, but I knew she was still about five minutes away. So I went sprinting down the hall, and I asked for a blank card without any flowers. I wrote something real sweet to Angie and put it on the flowers [and, of course, removed Charlie's card]. That was a nice arrangement of flowers."

Well, Charlie, if you're reading this book, make sure you bill a certain National League pitcher for those flowers. And make sure you add another five bucks or so for interest — he can afford it.

Storm and Angie were married on September 6, 1980, with First Baptist's well-known pastor, Dr. Homer Lindsay, Jr., performing the ceremony. Although each was only 18 years old, they don't necessarily believe in youthful marriages. "I think we were an exception," says Storm. Adds Angie, "Our parents felt good about it because of our relationship to the Lord. They didn't have any qualms about it, and both our sets of parents are very strict."

Storm makes it clear that his wife is a vital part of all he does. "Angie's a silent partner who stands back and is called 'Storm's wife' and yet takes it all in stride. Her mother has a lot of wisdom, and God has passed that down as Angie and her mother have studied the Scriptures together. She's a great listener; she listens to the problems I'm going through and she understands."

* * *

What does the long-range forecast hold for Storm Davis? His deepened spiritual life combined with his talent suggests a bright future — if he can be more consistent. Early in the 1986 season, Storm's four-hit win over Texas brought these words of praise from the Orioles' former manager, Earl Weaver: "He can dominate this league like Dwight Gooden dominates the National League. Maybe he was brought up too early. Twenty is awfully young, and he might just be maturing now."

Davis has changed leagues since Weaver made that comment, but the basic goal for Storm has not changed. "My desire to win is there," says Storm. "Angie would vouch for me on that. Even after I've given everything to God I go home and think about a game for an hour before I put it aside."

Yes, there's a drive to win, but also a strong sense of what is most important in life. "I know that whatever I do on the ball field or in my life I want to generate it all toward Jesus Christ," says Storm. "I know when they plant me in the ground that I'm going to step into the presence of Jesus, and whatever I've done for Him is the only thing that's going to matter."

So, once again, what does the future hold for Storm Davis? Maybe some All-Star appearances; maybe a Cy Young award; maybe more World Series action. Of course, there also could be arm trouble; other trades; unfulfilled potential.

But whatever the outcome, don't worry about Storm. Win or lose, he'll be just fine. He's put his life in the hands of a loving God, and he's got a loving wife by his side.

Orel Hershiser's name goes way back — he's the IVth to hold that handle — but he has some fresh insights on a modern problem.

11

OREL HERSHISER

He's From an Orel Tradition

When pitcher Orel Leonard Hershiser IV broke into the major leagues with the Los Angeles Dodgers, it wasn't just his executive-sounding name that confounded sportswriters. They also marveled at his manner, and at his innocence. There was something different about this guy. And it wasn't that he still collects bubble gum cards.

Steve Bisheff, writing in *The Sporting News 1986 Baseball Yearbook,* put it this way:

> If you didn't already know that No. 55 on the mound for the Los Angeles Dodgers was a legitimate major league baseball player, you'd swear that Richie Cunningham had donned spikes and double knits. No. 55 wouldn't, of course. He never swears. Nor does he smoke, drink, take drugs or bad-mouth reporters. Fact is, he doesn't

do much of anything except smile a lot and throw baseballs past the best hitters in the National League. Orel Leonard Hershiser is so clean his pitches almost squeak.

Or take it from columnist John Hall of the *Orange County (Calif.) Register:*

The inclination is to label No. 4 [referring to Orel's name] another Steve Garvey or Dale Murphy, except that he is even nicer — a totally refreshing package of bubbles and big dreams. Everybody does love No. 4, even the baseball writers. He doesn't smoke, doesn't drink, and lives by the Good Book, but he's no preacher and he's no shrinking violet. He's good copy. He's humorous, warm and friendly.

And Gordon Verrell, again in *The Sporting News 1986 Baseball Yearbook:*

On one hand we have Orel Leonard Hershiser IV — nice guy, devoted husband, proud father, Christian, product of good teaching and a strong family background. On the other hand we have Orel Hershiser, righthanded pitcher for the Los Angeles Dodgers. It's a combination that simply doesn't mix, insists the old-time baseball breed, the leathery, tobacco-chewing sort who say "When you step across that white line, it's war."

But with Hershiser, somehow it *does* mix.

After arriving in the majors to stay in 1984, Hershiser wasted no time getting the attention of the nation's media, not to mention National League batters. All Orel did as a rookie was:

•post a 2.66 earned run average;

•pitch four shutouts;

•put together a string of 34 consecutive scoreless innings.

Well, good grief, if the writers write about these things,

The eyes have it: No one questions "Bulldog" about his aggressiveness these days
PHOTO: CRAIG MOLLENHOUSE, LOS ANGELES DODGERS

why didn't they vote him Rookie of the Year? There was at least one good reason: Dwight Gooden happened to be a rookie the same year.

Hershiser may not have Gooden's ripping fastball, but he does have great movement on his fastball, two outstanding curves, and a sinker that drops off the table. "What makes him an outstanding pitcher is that he goes right at hitters," says former Dodger General Manager Al Campanis. "He's got poise. He's a competitor. He's got the demeanor of a winner."

"He also has one of the best curveballs in the league," says San Diego's Tony Gwynn, a former National League batting champ. "And he changes speed with it, too. That's what makes him so tough."

Hershiser is for real. He's obviously a great pitcher; he's proven that repeatedly, even with a slight slump in 1986. But what about that innocence the writers talk about? Is it for *real*?

Let's examine the evidence. First, the exterior. Yep, no question. The guy *looks* innocent. It's that face. Bright, boyish, friendly, right out of "Happy Days." So the exterior evidence checks out, and that's what most people go by, anyway.

But God doesn't go by outward appearances, and that brings our innocence check to the interior of the man. What about Orel Hershiser's heart?

Orel will be the first to tell you that while he's always looked innocent on the outside, he wasn't always on the inside. Until he experienced the miracle of forgiveness during his stay in the minor leagues, Orel's heart was dark, wrapped in sin.

Wow, that sounds pretty serious. It is, but don't get the wrong idea. Orel was your basic "great guy," certainly as good as any other person, and almost everybody liked him. He wasn't a doper, nor a drinker, and he didn't play around with sex (something he is very thankful for, as we'll see). But a person can act innocent and look innocent and still not be innocent before God. Orel learned that lesson during five long years in the minor leagues.

During Orel's youth, even the minor leagues seemed way beyond his reach. Back then, he had not only a baby face, but also a "baby body." To label him "thin" was generous. He was skinny, even emaciated. His chest was virtually nonexistent until about age 20.

Hershiser didn't make his high school baseball team until his junior year. Upon graduation, he had a total of one college scholarship offer — a partial ride to Bowling Green University in Ohio. After careful consideration for at least two minutes, he took it.

Orel became a pro prospect only after he underwent a growth spurt prior to his junior year. "I grew three inches over the summer," he says, "and gained 20 pounds. All of a sudden, instead of my fastball being 81 or 82 [miles-per-hour], it was now 85 or 86." The added zip gave him at least minor league, if not major league, ability. Thus, the Dodgers made Hershiser a seventeenth round draft choice after that junior season.

Still, says Orel, "I was more a suspect than a prospect."

The next five years were spent floundering in the Dodger system. They made Orel a relief pitcher, but that role didn't fit him well. Hershiser likes to look at the game as a whole, to set up hitters and work methodically. He couldn't do that as a reliever.

The rap on Hershiser in the minors was that he wasn't aggressive enough. People judged him by his baby face and not by the man inside. He was actually very intense, a fact demonstrated by his frustration at going nowhere in the Dodger minor league system. His frustration was so great that he couldn't enjoy the game, or much else.

Orel especially had trouble forgetting a bad performance. Instead, he tormented himself with questions: "Why did I throw that pitch? Why did I do that? Why did I lose?"

Hershiser tried everything to overcome his frustration. He even tried washing it away. "I thought I could shower it off," says Orel. "I took one after the game, then went home and couldn't sleep. So I thought, *A nice hot shower will relax me,* so I went and took another hot shower, got back in bed, and still couldn't sleep. Then I thought maybe I should take another one, a cold one. I was always looking for something to get me relaxed because I was so frustrated."

During this time, Orel began to get to know another pitcher on his team. The pitcher's name was Wicksheimer, and Wicksheimer was a Christian. The thing Orel liked about "Wicks" was that he knew Wicks really cared about him. Orel loved hanging around him, and Wicks looked after his younger friend. The two pitchers ended up being roommates. One day Wicks asked Orel if he was a Christian. Orel said, "Yes, I go to church on Christmas and Easter."

Wicksheimer said, "Then you know who Jesus Christ is."

"Yes, He's the one who died on the cross for our sins and we go to church to worship Him."

"But do you have a personal relationship with Him?"

Orel had to admit, "No, not really."

That day they talked about the meaning of sin, and man's (including Orel's) separation from God. Wicksheimer encouraged Orel to read the Gospel of John in the Bible. Orel did, and over the next two months he asked questions about the person of Jesus Christ. Orel finally concluded that he was a sinner and needed to accept the payment Christ made for his sins.

"It came down to 'When am I going to accept Him?' " says Orel. " 'When am I going to say "yes" to Him and turn my life over?' I didn't have the answers for eternity. I really didn't know what's going to happen after death. It came to a point where I knew this was the solution, and I finally bowed and said, 'I believe it, Lord; I know that I'm a sinner. I know that Your plan of salvation is that I believe in Your Son who died on the cross and rose from the dead, and that if I believe it I go to heaven.' And I said, 'I accept Your Son right now!' At that moment there were no bangs or whistles or fireworks. But I had peace and security and knew that I was going to heaven."

Within two to three months after his decision for Christ, Orel did something that perhaps other new Christians should consider. As a means of taking a stand for his new faith, he placed himself in a public position of Christian responsibility. "I did that through the organization Baseball Chapel," he says. "It was in San Antonio, Texas, AA ball, and I decided to be a chapel leader because I wanted to stand up for what I believe and be accountable. I became assistant chapel leader; I wouldn't take the actual leadership because I knew I wasn't strong enough." Suddenly, everyone was watching Orel Hershiser IV. There would be no turning back.

But to publicly proclaim Christ, Orel had to privately take care of some wrongs from his past. One of the first people he talked to was a former teammate. "When I was in A ball," says Orel, "I stole a baseball glove out of another guy's locker. He had about five of them, brand new gloves, and I had only one. After I became a Christian, I went back and gave him the glove and said, 'I'm sorry.' "

One of the biggest changes in Orel's life was that he

learned not to be frustrated by defeat. "God freed me up from that. Now I just go out and do my best during the contest and when I lose, I know I'll be fine. Before I became a Christian," he adds, "I got jealous of other players when they did well, but now God has freed me up just to do my best."

Hershiser's play gradually improved, and several times he was invited to the Dodgers' major league spring training camp in Vero Beach, Florida. Twice he was virtually the last man sent back to the minors ("not aggressive enough"), but finally in 1984 he hung on as the tenth man on a ten-man pitching staff.

As a rookie, Orel lacked confidence and was, in fact, about one more good pounding away from the minor leagues. It was then that Dodger Manager Tommy Lasorda called Orel into his office. Lasorda ripped into him with an exhortation that was, well, just what he needed to hear. "You're pitching to every hitter as if he was Babe Ruth!" said Lasorda, half-shouting. "You're giving these hitters too much credit. You don't believe you can get them out!"

Orel realized Lasorda was right. Major leaguers had been his heroes all his life, and now he was intimidated by them. He was trying not to make mistakes instead of aggressively going for outs.

Lasorda explains, "I just told him with the stuff he has he should go after every batter and not get behind [in the count]. Once he quit pitching like every guy he faced was Superman, he became a different pitcher." Lasorda also hung a nickname on Orel — "Bulldog" — to remind him to be aggressive.

It wasn't long before the rookie had a chance to show that he had learned his lesson. Regular starting pitcher Jerry Reuss was injured in May, 1984, and Lasorda brought Orel out of the bullpen to start against the Mets. Then, a month later, he earned a regular starting spot and won his first game with a shutout. That performance began the longest scoreless streak in the National League that year, and the rest, as they say, is history.

Having made it in the big-time, Hershiser's goals

remain simple. He wants to keep his ERA under 3.00, be a 20-game winner, and help the Dodgers win a World Series. But he also has a more important objective. "I think my number one professional goal is to be a good role model for the kids," Orel says. "With the cloud that's come over major league baseball with the drug problem, I figure that if the media can spotlight some of the players who stand up for the right things, and if the players can take the responsibility to the public to be role models and be considerate . . . well, I want to be available for that.

"Any exposure I get through baseball," continues Orel, "I want to use to glorify God. I hope that people know where the ability comes from. Also, I want to raise a successful family with my wife. If I have a successful home life, then I'm going to be a happy person."

Orel does have a very good relationship with his wife, Jamie, and it's based on principles from the Bible. "Jamie knows that I'm committed to her. She doesn't worry about me when I'm out on the road." Trust is a critical part of any relationship, and Orel says their trust was built on the foundation of not compromising standards *before* they married.

"The perfect plan is to have one wife," says Orel, "and not to have sex until you are married. I've found that is fantastic, that is the way to go."

But if sex is so fantastic and God is for it (and the Bible confirms He is), then why wait until marriage? Besides, isn't sex just a physical act? What's wrong with having sex with a girl, especially if you really love her?

Orel notes that sex is *not* just a physical relationship. "With sex you're establishing a relationship that is much deeper than a boyfriend-girlfriend commitment. Sex is also mental, emotional and spiritual."

Orel points out that sex can do great damage outside a permanent commitment. "It's just wrong before marriage," he says. "There's going to be a guilt feeling that comes with it." A lack of trust later in the relationship could be another result. A wife may be especially tempted to think, *If he bent the rules before marriage, he might do it again.*

Orel believes that since sex is God's idea, He says no about premarital sex to protect us and to provide a *maximum* sexual relationship after marriage. "I think God puts some boundaries on our lives, but only to protect us from getting hurt and causing hurt. It's just like when you're growing up as a little kid. Your parents tell you not to put your hand on a hot burner because you're going to get hurt. People resist that, but it's for their own good. In the same way, God knows what He's doing with sex."

Premarital sex, according to Hershiser, is not the way for a teenager to tell his girlfriend he loves her. First, he needs to learn to communicate with words — an important key to a good sexual relationship in marriage. Second, the young man who says, "Because I love you, I'll wait," demonstrates real love. True love, says Orel, is sacrificial. True love is patient.

The Hershiser philosophy says that if you are really in love with a girl, you should proclaim that love in a wedding ceremony. Give her the security she needs with a life-long commitment of marriage. *Then* enjoy the beautiful gift of sex God has given you for the rest of your lives.

But just as obvious as the need for self control is the fact that it's not so easy. What can a young man do to avoid sexual temptation? Orel Hershiser offers these principles that have helped him:

●*Watch your input.* Regulate what goes into your mind through TV, movies, and books. Avoid stimulating material, especially pornography. Replace the bad input with good, especially God's Word. As Proverbs 23:7 says, "As a man thinks within himself, so he is." Says Orel, "I try to filter those things out and not expose myself to things I know would be bad for me. When you're exposed to something bad and all of a sudden you realize it, that's when you need to turn away. I've gone to movies and walked out of them."

"When you become a Christian, the Holy Spirit comes into your life," says Orel. "When I became a Christian, the Holy Spirit started convicting me of sins. When I walked down the street there would be a bar on my left and I felt the Holy Spirit saying, 'Stay out of there! Stay out of there!' The more I listened to the Holy Spirit, the happier I became and the closer I felt to God."

●*Admit you're weak.* This honest admission will protect you by reminding you to keep out of the wrong situations. If you mistakenly think you are strong, you are more likely to find yourself in situations that will lead to sin. The Bible doesn't say to fight sexual sin; it says to flee it. "I stay away from the wrong establishments where I can get into trouble," says Orel, "also from the so-called 'groupies' and girls who are around major league teams."

●*Surround yourself with the right kind of people.* Young men usually develop an instinct to sense which girls are not of the highest moral standard. It's even easier for girls to sort out guys because a man who wants something physical is usually obvious about it. If you're serious about pleasing God, avoid the wrong types of people. "I hang around with people who believe the same things that I do," says Orel. "They strengthen me. If I hang around people who are trying to pull me away from what God wants, then I'm going to give in to that temptation."

●*Choose to obey God in every detail of your life.* Obedience is the key to the sexual area of one's life as it is in other areas. Hershiser advises, "Just get up in the morning and say, 'I'm going to say yes to the Holy Spirit today.' That is very tough to do, but I've found through spiritual growth that I've learned to say yes more and more." He also points out the connection between obedience and loving God. "How do you love God? You can't affectionately love God; you can't give Him a big hug, you can't kiss Him. But as it says in the Bible, we show our love for God by obeying Him."

Hershiser applies these principles in his life and continues to learn more through classes and Bible studies at his church in Fullerton, California. With these principles to protect him, and Christ's forgiveness making him innocent before God, Orel is free to fully enjoy life.

"I have a lot of fun being a Christian," he says. "In fact, I have more fun being a Christian than I did before because God has freed me up from so many things in the world that left me empty and dry. There's some pleasure to sin, yes, but I've found with my Christian walk the pleasure is more consistent and long-lasting."

Hershiser is indeed a fun-loving type. He doesn't even mind poking a little fun at his boss, Tommy Lasorda. Orel often tells the story about how Lasorda, famous for his love of food, finally decided to get in shape. "Tommy went out and bought a rowing machine," says the ace pitcher. "But the first time he used it, it sank!"

Be careful, Orel. If Lasorda hears about your taste in humor, he may call you into his office for another loud discussion. And when Tommy's temper gets fired up, even *you* won't be able to keep an innocent look on your face.

One of baseball's most powerful hitters has also shown plenty of spiritual power, especially when faced with tragedy.

12

ANDRE THORNTON

The Pain and the Glory

Relaxing in the Cleveland Indians' locker room before a game, Andre Thornton looks like he was poured into his T-shirt. It's not that he has chosen a size too small. They just don't make T-shirts big enough. The man is muscular, having trained with Nautilus weights since the early 1970s.

Thornton's soft voice and gentle manner are the first indicators of a different kind of strength. Strength of character. That strength has been formed in him by God and refined by suffering.

But in baseball, strength means power, and power means the ability to hit the long ball. Thornton has done that well, launching more than two hundred home runs in his career. He's homered twice in the same game more than a dozen times. "I think he's the strongest man in baseball right now," says Cleveland hitting coach Tom

McGraw. "When I see Andy hit home runs, I'm thinking Harmon Killebrew. Balls that go four miles up, then out. Hank Aaron hit line drives — shots. But with Andy, outfielders keep going back and back, thinking they have a chance, and then the ball ends up 150 feet deeper."

Thornton is one of the most respected players in the major leagues, and not just because he's a premier performer. It's because of the way he lives his life. Andre may be the only star in the major leagues who is perhaps better known as a Christian than as a ballplayer.

"The thing I like about Andre," says writer Paul Hoynes, who covers the Indians for the *Cleveland Plain Dealer,* "is that he's a Christian but he doesn't wear it on his sleeve. There's nothing phony about him. He's very sincere. When you ask him what pitch he hit he doesn't tell you, 'God made me hit that.' They named him captain, so I'd say he's the most respected player on the team."

Thornton frequently hears the question: "Can you play tough as a Christian?" The notion is that a Christian can't crash into a pivoting second baseman to break up a double play.

"People ask me about that," says Andre. "It's as if they assume you can't be aggressive if you love the Lord. What malarkey! Why do we think a man has to curse or drink to be a tough player? I can do my job just as intensely and aggressively as anyone, even with the love of God flowing through me.

"It's the intent of a man's heart that matters. I've been knocked down. I've been hit. And I've broken up my share of double plays. I've done it because it's my job. But I don't do it with murder in my heart.

"Is it drinking and cursing that makes you a tough ballplayer? Of course not. It's talent that distinguishes players, but what separates some good ballplayers from the great ones is their inability to cope with this life, even though they may have all the talent they need."

Coping with life. That means overcoming the problems that life hands us and still going on to find fulfillment and meaning. That takes character — something Andre

It's outta here: Andre watches long blast before rounding the bases
COURTESY CLEVELAND INDIANS

Thornton has lots of today. When he was young, however, Thornton lacked what he needed to cope with life's problems.

Andre grew up in Phoenixville, Pennsylvania, a river

town west of Philadelphia. His mother and father worked
hard and loved Andre. But his father had one vice — alcoholism. The Thorntons lived in a tough neighborhood.
Many of the families were Black Muslims. From them,
Andre learned a lot about the Black Muslim view of the
white man's world.

One of seven children, Andre was a hostile person
with a nasty outlook on life. He hated what he saw in
society — racism, injustice, lies. People talked about the
American Dream, but to him that was a lie. The Vietnam
War had heated up and Andre's friends were coming
back maimed.

Death also troubled him. One of his older brothers
died when Andre was a child. One of his best friends
was stabbed to death. Andre himself almost drowned in
the Schuylkill River, tumbling over and over in the black
water below a dam before making it to shore. A grade
school friend later drowned in that same spot. A man
was shot to death a few houses down the street. Another
man was killed while walking on the railroad tracks that
ran just 35 yards from his house.

"I was particularly troubled by the deaths," Andre
says. "I questioned why anyone had to die. I wondered
what happened to us after we die. And I wondered why
we were here on earth. No one seemed to be able to
answer those questions to my satisfaction."

As a teenager, Thornton was kicked out of school for
smoking. The police picked him up a couple of times
for fighting. His hang-out was the local pool hall, where
Andre often spent 14 to 16 hours a day. That's where he
made his lunch money and the money to buy his class
ring. The pool hall was near an Army base, and he and
the owner had a deal. The owner let him play for nothing
and Andre cut him in on what he won in bets. As
Thornton once said in a conversation with writer Terry
Pluto, "I did pretty well because the soldiers thought
they could play. I would look for guys who thought they
were sharks. You can win big against guys like that. I
was a good player. I could run 80 to 82 balls in straight
pool."

Thornton was a three-sport (basketball, football and baseball) star in high school. But football was the only one that really mattered to him — the contact provided a way for him to take out his aggressions on opponents. He looked forward to playing college football somewhere.

But that was before a Philadelphia Phillies scout named John Ogden found him. Ogden, 72 years old at the time, found Thornton at the pool hall (where else?) in the middle of a game of nine-ball, playing for a $300 pot. The scout changed Andre's mind about college football. Thornton signed with the Phillies and, at 17, ventured north to Huron, South Dakota, to begin the long climb toward the major leagues.

The Phillies, to keep Andre in the States and out of Vietnam, recommended that he join the National Guard. The move effectively protected him from the military draft. But during National Guard boot camp at Fort Dix, New Jersey, something more significant happened. It was there that Thornton finally found answers to his troubling questions.

"It was one of the loneliest times of my life," he says of boot camp. "Everything seemed so confusing, and questions about life were boiling inside me. It wasn't money I was looking for. It wasn't clothes or houses or a profession that had prestige. I wanted to know what life was all about. Why was I here? Where was I going? Here I was, experiencing all the things that most people want, but the world could not give the true answers that I needed so urgently."

One night, sitting alone in the barracks, Andre picked up a Salvation Army leaflet that his mother had given him. "She had become a Christian when I was 11 years old," Andre says of his mother, "but I hadn't followed her example."

In the leaflet, he read that God had a plan for his life. For the first time, he understood Christ's words: "I came that they might have life and might have it abundantly" (John 10:10). Says Thornton, "I knew that was what I was looking for — life, abundant life. Here was the answer to my question. First, God had a purpose for my life. He created me in order that I might enjoy Him and serve Him. But the reason I didn't understand His purpose was that I was spiritually dead. The Bible told me that 'all have sinned and fall short of the glory of God' (Romans 3:23), and that 'the wages of sin is death' (Romans 6:23), which means spiritual separation from God.

"Then I read that there was a solution to this problem. The key was believing in God's Son, Jesus Christ. The Bible says, 'God has given us eternal life, and this life is in His Son. He who has the Son has the life; he who does not have the Son of God does not have the life. These things are written to you who believe in the name of the Son of God, in order that you may *know* that you have eternal life' (1 John 5:11-13)."

In response to those words, Andre got down on his knees in the barracks and prayed: "Lord Jesus, I know I am a sinner. Please forgive me of my sins. Thank you for dying for me, and for coming back to life three days later. Please take my life and do what You want with it. Help me not to be afraid of death."

"Now that I had the answers to those questions," says Andre, "I doubted if they were real. It sounded good, but could I trust it and believe it? The answer to that came as I looked at my mother and noticed the changes God had made in her life. I saw her peace as she had to cope with my alcoholic father, and with raising seven children. As I studied her life, I realized that God could be trusted to work in my life, too."

As Christ worked in Andre's life, the hatred and hopelessness disappeared. But that didn't mean the end of difficulties.

First, there was baseball. Thornton had to labor seven long years in the minor leagues before making the big time. In one six-year period, he played for nine different teams, creating the kind of uncertainty that would hurt anyone's performance. Philadelphia traded Thornton to Atlanta, Atlanta to the Chicago Cubs, the Cubs to the Expos, and the Expos sent him to Cleveland, where he finally found a semi-permanent address.

But even tougher than continually loading up the moving van were the injuries. Andre often found himself on the disabled list. Right after the Cubs swapped Thornton to the Expos he was struck by a pitch and broke his wrist. He batted only .193 that season. Another time with the Indians his knee buckled during a spring training game and he damaged cartilage. He had surgery and pushed himself hard to rehabilitate the knee. He was supposed to be back in the lineup after two months but the knee wasn't ready. Some people in management implied that Thornton was loafing and didn't want to play. That hurt. But he forgave them because of his convictions as a Christian.

Andre continued to work during that winter to build up the injured knee. When he reported to training the following spring he was in great condition. But in the first exhibition game against the Tayio Whales of Japan, he was hit in the hand by a pitch that broke his thumb. Again, Thornton found himself back on the disabled list.

He was reactivated in May and he batted at a torrid pace for three weeks. For a while, the Indians were in first place. Then came a players' strike. Three weeks after the strike was settled, Thornton stretched ligaments in his thumb while trying to halt a brawl between the Tribe and the California Angels.

"Why?" That might be a logical response after one has suffered so many setbacks. But Thornton doesn't ask that question and doesn't think he's been singled out by God to suffer unfairly. "Suffering is for everyone," says Andre. "The difference for believers is that we have help for the suffering. Where the nonbeliever is left many times with no help, we have help.

"I remember a verse that spoke very dearly to my heart. It was Romans 8:18: '. . . the suffering of this present time cannot be compared with the glory that is to be revealed to us.' So the Lord reminds us that yes, we're going to suffer but it's not even comparable to the glory we'll experience one day with Him. The Lord reminds us, too, that trials bring forth patience and character."

It's obvious that Andre takes the Bible very seriously. That was the foundation that took him through his greatest trial, one far worse than any injury, as we'll see shortly. Andre has systematically studied the Bible since becoming a Christian. "We're commanded to read the Word," says Andre. "We're told that the Word is our source of food, our source of strength. Certainly we cannot know what God wants us to do if we don't read His Word . . . So the Bible is our manual, our source of strength, our direction, our instruction. But more than that, it's our hope because it reminds us of the hope that we have in Christ as believers."

It was the years of training from God's Word that enabled Andre to respond in faith when he faced a most severe form of suffering. One night shortly after the 1977 season, Andre and his wife, a lovely Christian woman named Gert, left Cleveland to drive to Gert's sister's wedding. The Thorntons and their two children, Andre Jr. and Theresa, were driving along an icy Pennsylvania Turnpike when suddenly their van skidded out of control. There was nothing Andre could do, it happened so fast. The crash killed Gert and two-year-old Theresa.

A pastor drove the two survivors from Somerset Hospital to West Chester, Pennsylvania, where Andre's in-laws lived. The major leaguer sat in shock throughout the four-hour trip. The most traumatic moment was when the hearse from the funeral home passed by, going the other way. Andre knew it would pick up the bodies of his loved ones. He broke down and wept.

The days that followed are still a blur to him. He remembers people coming by . . . telephone calls and telegrams from around the country . . . condolences from every major league team.

The night before the funeral, Andre's mother called him and said, "Andre, I dreamed last night that I should give you this verse — 1 Peter 1:25, 'The Word of the Lord endures forever.' " At first he didn't understand the significance of that particular verse. But that night, he slowly read the entire chapter and saw the great comfort he could gain from Scripture:

All honor to God, the God and Father of our
Lord Jesus Christ; for it is His boundless mercy
that has given us the privilege of being born
again, so that we are now members of God's
own family. Now we live in the hope of eternal
life because Christ rose from the dead. And God
has reserved for His children the priceless gift of
eternal life; it is kept in heaven for you, pure
and undefiled, beyond the reach of change and
decay. And God, in His mighty power, will make
sure that you get there safely to receive it, because
you are trusting in Him. It will be yours in that
coming last day for us all to see. *So be truly
glad! There is wonderful joy ahead, even though
the going is rough for a while down here.*

These trials are only to test your faith, to see
whether or not it is strong and pure. It is being
tested as fire tests gold and purifies it — and
your faith is far more precious to God than mere
gold; so if your faith remains strong after being
tried in the test tube of fiery trials, it will bring
you much praise and glory and honor on the
day of His return (1 Peter 1:3-7, Living Bible).

Andre continued praying that night and God gave
him a strong desire to share his hope with all those who
would be at the funeral the next day. God seemed to
be telling Andre to speak at the service.

The next morning, the Bethel A.M.E. Church was
packed to capacity. It was an emotional service. Andre
Jr.'s grief was too much for him; he leaned against his
father and quietly cried himself to sleep.

When the pastor finished speaking, Andre woke his
son and took him by the hand. Together they stood in
front of the congregation. Tears flowed from Andre's
eyes, but he was able to speak these words: "There are
tears in my eyes, but my heart is comforted. The reason
I'm standing here now is because you knew Gert and
Theresa, and you know what our lives represented. You
know how we tried to live our lives for the Lord. We

thank God for giving us a chance to touch as many lives as He made possible.

"Today, these tears you see are not for me. These tears are for you, and I pray that before one of your lives is stolen away, before another person here passes away, each one of you will ask Jesus Christ into your life and know Him as your Savior."

People later asked Andre when he first felt God's peace. He could tell them that he felt God's peace from the first moments of the tragedy. "There is no doubt that the accident was like tearing the insides right out of me," says Andre. "Gert was a wonderful woman. We spent seven years together. I felt God's presence right there on the highway in Pennsylvania. I felt God's peace. It wasn't something that was only printed in a Bible verse; it was real. Now I'm thankful that I knew Him years before, that I didn't have to come to that point in my life and have no hope at all . . . Hope is the essence of life."

Andre knew that his son needed a mother and eventually began to pray that God would bring the right person into his life. God did. Dr. Howard Jones, an associate evangelist with Billy Graham, lived near Cleveland and had prayed with Andre as he suffered through the agony. He invited Andre to his home two months after the tragedy and there Andre met one of Dr. Jones's daughters, Gail, an airline stewardess who was home for the holidays. Andre and Gail became friends and talked almost daily by phone. It soon became clear that she was God's provision for Andre and Andre Jr. And vice-versa, of course, as well. Andre and Gail were married on November 4, 1978, a year after the accident.

In the years since, they've added two children to their family, Jonathan David and Dean Michael. And their family life together is based on principles from the same book that comforted Andre during his time of grief. They want to share those Bible principles with people who need God's strength for family living, especially in the inner cities of North America. Therefore, Andre and Gail and others in the extended Jones family have founded

"Christian Family Outreach."

For now, however, Andre and Gail's prime ministry involves those they can reach in and through baseball. "We [Christians] must remember what kind of message we're giving," says Andre. "We're giving the life-giving message to a dying world."

Despite death and discrimination, there is hope in that world. Ask Andre Thornton. He has suffered in the valley, but emerged victorious.

It took a special form of courage for Dodger executive Branch Rickey and infielder Jackie Robinson to stand up against segregation in baseball.

13

BRANCH RICKEY
and JACKIE ROBINSON

When Faith Smashed
the Color Barrier

Of all the unusual personalities ever produced in baseball, no one matches the late Branch Rickey, Sr. Not Casey Stengel. Not Leo Durocher. Not George Steinbrenner. Rickey stands alone. That's not to say that Rickey was some sort of empty-headed flake. Far from it. The old gentleman held a law degree from the University of Michigan and could easily be described as an intellectual, philosopher, teacher and religious leader.

It's just that Rickey never felt the need to be ordinary. Always eloquent, he once stated a problem this way: "I have come to the point of a cliff. I stand poised at the precipice. Earth crumbles. My feet slip. I am tumbling over the edge. Certain death lies below. Only one man can save me. Who is that man?"[1] The problem? Rickey needed a good relief pitcher.

Rickey was a baseball genius who served as chief

executive for several teams between 1917 and 1955. As general manager of the St. Louis Cardinals, he built the sport's first farm system, and he continued to cultivate the farm with the Brooklyn Dodgers and Pittsburgh Pirates. He introduced sliding pits and batting tees. He emphasized speed and urged his players toward "Adventure!" on the basepaths long before the Vince Coleman/ Rickey Henderson era.

Rickey used expressions like "Balzac!", had thick and bushy eyebrows, and as a young man, he proposed to his sweetheart about 100 times before she agreed to marry him.[2] Veteran sportswriter Red Smith, who knew Rickey for many years, described him this way: "a player, manager, executive, lawyer, preacher, horse-trader, spellbinder, innovator, husband and father and grandfather, farmer, logician, obscurantist, reformer, financier, sociologist, crusader, sharper, father confessor, checker shark, friend and fighter."[3]

* * *

It was fortunate for baseball that Rickey was willing to be different. Without his high ideals and courage, the ugliest sin in baseball might have lasted much longer. That sin was the "color barrier," the wall that once kept blacks from playing in the major leagues.

It seems hard to imagine there was once a time when Willie Mays would have been barred from organized baseball by athletic apartheid. It seems inconceivable that just 40 years ago, men like Hank Aaron, Dave Winfield and Dwight Gooden would have been told privately, "If only you were white . . ."

Oh, a few blacks had played in the big leagues during the 1800s, but the big leagues weren't really so big then — not with teams in Topeka, Binghamton, Toledo, and Syracuse. By 1892, however, the color barrier was firmly in place. Not until 1947, when Branch Rickey stuck his neck out, would another black player appear on a major league roster.

The owners didn't want to admit to segregation, so

History is made: Jackie Robinson (left) signs with Branch Rickey to become major league baseball's first black player
PHOTO: UPI

they claimed that black stars like Satchel Paige, Josh Gobson and Cool Papa Bell didn't have the "polish" to compete with white players. If so, maybe Ty Cobb and Babe Ruth also lacked polish.

Black players did their thing in the Negro Leagues, and many of them said they were happy on teams like the Kansas City Monarchs, Homestead Grays, and Pittsburgh Crawfords. But most of the teams stayed in horrible hotels or used their buses as dining room, locker room, and hotel. And always there was that gnawing desire in a black player's heart to prove that he could play with the best. "We always played the major leaguers [in off-season exhibitions]," said one black player, "and we knew that there wasn't any difference because we used to always beat 'em."[4]

Branch Rickey first experienced baseball segregation in 1903. Just 21 years old, he was serving as baseball coach for his college, Ohio Wesleyan University, which had a black player, Charles Thomas. In Rickey's first game as coach, the opposing players got one look at Thomas and said they wouldn't play if he did.

Imagine how you might have felt in Rickey's position when the other team began to yell, "Get that nigger boy off the field!" But even as a rookie coach in his first game, Rickey's convictions showed through. He walked over to the opponents' bench, pointed a finger at their coach and shouted, "You will play Charles Thomas or you don't play OWU."

The future major league executive then ordered his players to toss the ball around so they could stay loose. They certainly played lots of catch that day, for the matter wasn't decided for an hour. Finally, the visitors agreed to play. Rickey had stood his ground and won as a 21-year-old.

But this one victory wouldn't strike the ugly word "nigger" from America's vocabulary, and Charles Thomas continued to feel the nasty slap of racism. The very next season, for example, Rickey's OWU team was in South Bend, Indiana, to play Notre Dame. The team had made reservations to stay in the Oliver Hotel, but the hotel manager just about swallowed his choppers when he saw Charles Thomas in the lobby. The manager declared that only whites were welcome at the Oliver. Deeply hurt, Thomas offered to return directly to OWU, but Rickey refused his offer. Instead, he ordered a cot to be put in his own room and insisted that Thomas be allowed to share the room. "Under no circumstances," he said firmly, "will I leave or allow Thomas to be put out."

Rickey had won another victory, but Charles Thomas wasn't throwing anyone in the showers to celebrate. Years later, Rickey recalled his reaction this way: "We went upstairs. I summoned the captain to discuss plans for the game, Tommy stood in the corner, tense and brooding and in silence . . . I tried to talk to our captain, but I couldn't take my gaze from Tommy. Tears welled in the large, staring eyes. They spilled down his black face and splashed to the floor. Then his shoulders heaved convulsively, and he rubbed one great hand over the other

with all the power of his body, muttering, 'Black skin
. . . black skin. If I could only make 'em white.' "

Rickey felt the impact of every tear. He later said,
"For 40 years I've had recurrent visions of him wiping
off his skin."[5]

Perhaps without Charles Thomas in his memory,
Branch Rickey would not have been as willing to endure
the struggles of the 1940s when he broke baseball's color
barrier. But Rickey's desire to change baseball's racial
climate also stemmed from his Christian faith.

The Ohio native grew up in a family of deeply committed Christians — some Baptists, some Methodists. He
took the Christian faith into his own heart at an early
age. Many students at Christian colleges dreaded chapel
services even in Rickey's day, but he was different. At
OWU, "chapel thrilled Rickey though others stayed away
when they could."[6] Years later, when tragic headlines
worried others about the world's fate, Rickey had a rock
to hold onto. "This will abide," he would say of the Bible.[7]

Rickey's faith influenced his entire lifestyle. It gave
him a deep love for his family. It caused him to warn
others constantly about the dangers of alcohol — even
when they mocked him for being puritanical. It caused
him to want to influence others for Christ (he helped to
begin the Fellowship of Christian Athletes). It led him
to seek the welfare of others.

And Rickey's faith led him to set his bespectacled face
squarely against segregation in baseball. "I couldn't face
my God much longer knowing that His black creatures
are held separate and distinct from His white creatures
in the game that has given me all I own," he once said.[8]

Thus, the Dodger leader made a decision that would
shake America's pastime to its foundation. He would
bring a black player to the Dodgers, but he would do
so only with careful planning.

First, the timing was critical, and with the end of
World War II, Rickey felt America was finally ready for
such a change. Blacks had fought side-by-side with
whites, and now some of those same whites were more
willing to live in a mixed culture. They also realized that

the evil they had been battling — Nazi Germany — was based on the faulty idea of one race's superiority over others.

Second, Rickey knew he must have the solid backing of his club's owners, and this seemed to be falling in place in the mid-40s, especially when Mr. John L. Smith, another "fervent Christian," became one of the Dodgers' owners.

Third, Rickey knew the right athlete must be found. Like NASA's original astronauts, this man would have to have the "right stuff." He would have to be a gifted athlete, of course, and he would have to be plenty tough to withstand the beanballs and body blocks that would come his way. He would have to be intelligent, articulate and morally upright so that bigoted critics would not be able to get to first base when trying to blast him. And he would have to be willing to receive abuse without returning it. To fight back would play into the hands of his enemies and ruin Rickey's "Grand Experiment."

Always a talent hawk, Rickey never lacked for good scouts, and they found a player named Jackie Robinson. Of course, Robinson really didn't require much finding. Most any sports fan in California knew about this splendid athlete. At UCLA, Jackie starred in football, basketball, track and baseball. Twice he led the Pacific Coast Conference (now Pacific 10) in basketball scoring. As a football halfback, he averaged a whopping 11 yards per carry in his junior year and earned All-American honors. In track, he won the National Collegiate Athletic Association championship for the long jump, and he hit .466 one baseball season.

But Robinson didn't stop with those four sports. He dabbled at golf and won the Pacific Coast title; he also won swimming championships. And in tennis, he reached the semifinals of the national Negro tournament.

Yes, Jackie Robinson had the physical talent to break the color barrier in major league baseball. And he also was no stranger to the racial slurs he would encounter, although he grew up in Pasadena, California. At age 14, Jackie went wading in the Pasadena Reservoir because of a ban against blacks using the municipal pool. Someone saw him splashing, called law enforcement authorities, and a few minutes later Jackie looked at one of the ugliest and most fearful sights of his life. A sheriff was pointing a gun at him and yelling, "Looka here. Nigger in my drinking water."[9]

Despite this and many similar events, Jackie never allowed his spirit to be broken. Branch Rickey, reading his scouting reports carefully, admired Robinson's strength but worried that perhaps he might be too defiant. While a lieutenant in the Army, Robinson defied a Southern bus driver's order to sit in the back of the bus. Aware that the Army had recently ordered military buses desegregated, Robinson refused. A court martial followed, but Jackie was cleared. Yes, Jackie Robinson had enough spirit to break baseball's color barrier, but could he walk the emotional tightrope which is required of a racial pioneer? Or would he lash out in rage and ruin his cause?

* * *

The two men met in Rickey's Brooklyn office on August 28, 1945. Robinson, brought to the city by scout Clyde Sukeforth, thought he was being considered for an all-black team, but Rickey stunned him. "I brought you here to play for the Brooklyn Dodgers — if you can!" he told Robinson.

The older man asked Jackie if he had a girlfriend and was pleased to hear that the Kansas City Monarch infielder would soon be married. Soon, though, he got to the central point of the interview. Could Robinson keep his cool when fans, opponents or even his own teammates called him a black so-and-so? "Mr. Rickey," answered Jackie, "I think I can play ball, but I promise you that I will do the second part of the job [avoiding fights], although I can't be an obsequious, cringing fellow."[10]

The UCLA man definitely spoke Rickey's language with a two-dollar word like "obsequious," and the Dodger leader was delighted at his polished speech. But he knew how much racial abuse Robinson would receive, and he wasn't yet convinced of the Californian's self-control.

Never the shy type, Rickey began to portray some of the big league bigots that Robinson could expect to meet.

"Look me in the eye," he said. "Now I'm a hotel clerk in some lousy dump where they won't like you." His kindly face took on a hateful glare. "You can't stay here," he yelled. "You want to be white? What you doing this for? Answer me!"

"I don't want to be white," replied Jackie. "I just want to play big league ball."

Next, Rickey portrayed a young tough, perhaps a fan or an opposing player. "A nigger is a nigger and that's all he'll ever be — just a nigger," he roared. "Well, what've you got to say?" As Robinson began to answer, Rickey kicked him in the shin to see if his emotions would stand up under the pressure.

Jackie's eyes lit with anger; his fists clenched. Rickey later said he wondered if an attack might follow.

But Robinson dropped his hands. "I don't want to make any trouble," he said to the "young tough." "I just came here to play ball."[11]

The historic meeting lasted three hours. Rickey told Robinson that he would hear some ugly things on the field — not to mention what his future bride, Rachel, would hear in the stands.

And he reminded the gifted black athlete that he probably would be treated rougher than any rookie in history. "Suppose," said Rickey, "a player comes down from first base — you are the shortstop — the player slides, spikes high, and cuts you on the leg. As you feel the blood running down your leg, the white player laughs in your face, and sneers, 'How do you like that, nigger boy?' "

Said Robinson, "Mr. Rickey, are you looking for a Negro who is afraid to fight back?"

"Robinson, I'm looking for a ballplayer with guts enough *not* to fight back!" Rickey reached into his desk drawer and brought out *The Life of Christ* by Giovanni Papini, an Italian who was once famous as an atheist but who had experienced a stunning conversion. He began to quietly read some famous words of Jesus from Matthew 5 and Papini's related comments:

> *"Ye have heard that it hath been said, An eye for an eye, and a tooth for a tooth: But I say unto you, that ye resist not evil: But whosoever shall smite thee on the right cheek, turn to him the other also . . ."*
>
> Every man has an obscure respect for courage in others, especially if it is moral courage, the rarest and most difficult sort of bravery. It makes the very brute understand that this man is more than a man . . . the results of nonresistance, even if they are not always perfect, are certainly superior to those of resistance or flight . . . To answer blows with blows, evil deeds with evil deeds, is to meet the attacker on his own ground, to proclaim oneself as low as he . . . Only he who has conquered himself can conquer his enemies.

Rickey placed the book down. "Now," he said to Robinson, "can you do it? You will have to promise that for the first three years in baseball you will turn your other cheek . . . Three years — can you do it?"

"Mr. Rickey," said Jackie Robinson, "I've got two cheeks. Is that it?"[12]

* * *

Rickey felt Robinson could use a year to prepare physically and mentally for the big leagues. On October 23, 1945, Jackie Robinson signed a contract for the '46 season to play with Brooklyn's top farm team, the Montreal Royals. It proved to be a good move. Canadians, somewhat removed from the racial problems of America, quickly received Robinson as a hero. Jackie's manager, a Mississippi native named Clay Hopper, was not such an instant admirer, however.

Rickey later told of Hopper's initial reaction to Robinson, which Rickey observed during a 1946 spring training game: "In the seventh inning, Jackie (playing second base) made one of those tremendous and remarkable plays that very few people can make . . . I took Clay and I put my hand on his shoulder and I said, 'Did you ever see a play to beat it?' Now this fellow comes from Greenwood, Mississippi. And he took me and shook me [with] his face that far from me and he said, 'Do you really think that a nigger is a human being, Mr. Rickey?' . . . I never answered him."[13]

Nor did Rickey need to answer Hopper. "Six months later," according to Rickey, "he came into my office after the year in Montreal . . . 'I want to take back what I said to you last spring,' he said. 'I'm ashamed of it. Now, you may have plans for him to be on your club but if you don't have plans to have him on the Brooklyn club, I would like to have him back at Montreal. He was not only a great ballplayer good enough for Brooklyn, but also a fine gentleman.' "[14]

Though a perfect gentleman in Montreal, Robinson treated opposing pitchers unkindly. He topped the International League in hitting (.349 average) and in runs scored (113) and led the Royals to the league title. Then, as if to suit a Hollywood script, Jackie and his teammates defeated the Louisville Colonels of the American Association in the Little World Series, the championship of the minor leagues.

He played somewhat poorly during the games in Louisville, where some of the fans rudely greeted him with terms like "watermelon eater," but he was a hero in Montreal. After the title was captured, ecstatic Montreal fans lifted Robinson to their shoulders and cheered him in both English and French while tears appeared in his eyes. Later, when he attempted to leave the stadium, the crowd chased him for three blocks. "It was probably the only day in history," wrote reporter Sam Maltin, "that a black man ran from a white mob with love, instead of lynching on its mind."[15]

Clearly, Jackie was ready for the Dodgers. But big league ball meant big league bigotry, so both Robinson and Rickey knew that the 1947 season would be the greatest challenge of their lives. Could Jackie hold up under the constant abuse he would receive?

And how about Mr. Rickey? Could he cope with the attacks of reporters who had already labelled him as greedy and a religious goody-goody? Already in his mid-60s and suffering from a nervous disorder called Meniere's Disease, could he cope with attacks against himself and also support Robinson?

The first major test came from within Dodger ranks. Several of the players passed around a petition that stated they would not play for Brooklyn if a black man did. The movement might have become a major threat to Robinson except for one man, Pee Wee Reese. A native Kentuckian who had probably never shaken a black man's hand, Reese was expected to side with Jackie's foes. But he chose not to rock Rickey's boat for fear of being traded or cut. "I wasn't trying to think of myself as the Great White Father," the Dodger captain later said. "I just wanted to play the game, especially after being in the Navy [during World War II] and needing the money."[16] Reese later became Robinson's closest friend on the team and his golfing buddy.

The Dodger protest ended quickly, but opposing teams did not exactly roll out the red carpet for Robinson. Take the Phillies for example. First, their general manager said he feared a riot by fans if Robinson came with the Dodgers to play ball in Philadelphia. "We're just not ready for that sort of thing yet," the GM told Rickey. "We won't be able to take the field with your Brooklyn team if that boy Robinson is in uniform."

Rickey must have felt like he was back in 1903 with a player named Thomas rather than Robinson. At any rate, he was ready with a firm reply. "If we must claim the game 9-0 [the score for any forfeit], we will do just that, I assure you," he said.[17]

Robinson played the Phillies, but he probably wished he hadn't. Led by their manager, Ben Chapman, the Phils of 1947 yelled all sorts of ugly things about Robinson and his wife, and they told the other Dodgers not to touch Jackie's towels or comb if they wanted to avoid disease.

It was not a pretty chapter in baseball history, but now some of the Dodgers who had once opposed Jackie were seen defending him. They found themselves admiring his quiet strength.

Baseball commissioner Happy Chandler took action to limit filthy bench jockeying, not only in Philadelphia but throughout the National League. But problems persisted. The St.Louis Cardinals might have boycotted their games with the Dodgers if the news of this possibility had not become public in advance. Warned of the problem, National League President Ford Frick told Cardinal owner Sam Braedon what to say to his players. "Tell them," said Frick, "that this is America and baseball is America's game. Tell them that if they go on strike, for racial reasons . . . they will be barred from baseball even though it means the disruption of a club or a whole league."[18] You guessed it . . . no strike in St. Louis.

And then there were the death threats. Robinson received enough of them that Rickey finally had the Dodger office open all his mail. Scheduled to take part in an exhibition game in Atlanta, Robinson received a letter from the Ku Klux Klan stating that he'd be shot if he played. Pee Wee Reese couldn't resist the chance to tease his friend. During warm-ups he said, "Jack, don't stand so close to me today. Move away, will ya?"[19]

The first season took a heavy toll on both Rickey and Robinson. Jackie may have even been near a nervous breakdown. His wife, Rachel, said, "I tried again and again to get him to talk, but he didn't want to burden me. He never would talk about those things at home. But I knew they were eating at his mind, for he would jerk and twitch and even talk in his troubled sleep."[20]

Rickey, meanwhile, got his share of flak from other baseball executives — and plenty of hate mail. As a result, he was troubled more than ever by his nervous disease, suffering constant spells of dizziness and nausea. But despite his own problems, Rickey and his wife, Jane, reached out to the Robinsons — inviting them to their home, taking them on a picnic, reminding them from the Bible of Job's patience during trials.

"We called him often," said Rachel, "because we needed support in this. We knew that Mr. Rickey was always there, always responsive; there was a consistency in his supprt. He didn't back off when things got tough."[21]

The victory was obvious, both in Jackie's performance and in the fan response. He hit .297 that first season, led the league in stolen bases ("Adventure!"), won the Rookie of the Year award and helped take the Dodgers to the World Series where they lost to the Yankees in seven games. Later years brought further success, including the Most Valuable Player award in 1949, when Jackie hit .342; and a World Series crown for the Dodgers in 1955. As for the fans, folks both white and black responded to Robinson. A national poll taken at the end of 1947 revealed him to be America's second most popular figure. Only Bing Crosby was more popular.[22]

And so the "Grand Experiment" proved to be a grand slam success. Not only did other blacks follow Robinson to the Dodgers (such as Roy Campanella and Don Newcombe), but Larry Doby soon signed with Cleveland to become the first black player in the American League. In just a few years many major league teams had at least one black player. This was about seven years before the Supreme Court ruled against segregation in America's schools.

Rickey, of course, was thrilled, and he gave credit to Jackie. "Surely, God was with me when I picked Jackie," he later said. "I don't think any other man . . . could have done what he did those first two or three years . . ."[23]

Robinson, meanwhile, never stopped expressing his sincere thanks to the Dodger boss. He said, "I really believe that in breaking down the color barrier in baseball, our 'national game,' [Branch Rickey] did more for the Negroes than any white man since Abraham Lincoln."[24]

Yes, Rickey had done something noble, but he frequently reminded people that it was his Christian faith which had moved him to sign Robinson. That makes sense when you read these words which he wrote in his 20s: "Power to make others happy is the greatest asset in the world, I think. We must believe in the doctrine of 'Loving God and one's brothers.' Jesus Christ made people happy just by loving them . . ."[25]

The conclusion is simple. It was the courage of Jackie Robinson that broke baseball's color barrier. But it was Branch Rickey, putting his Christian faith into action, who gave him his chance. Baseball owes them both a great debt.

Christianity does not bar aggressive play, but it does enhance the enjoyment of the game, and all of life.

14

HOW FAITH AFFECTS MAJOR LEAGUERS

The Christian movement in baseball stands for faith in Christ, obviously, but where does that faith lead? In general, how does Christianity affect athletes in their attitudes toward their profession, toward other people, even toward themselves?

•*Born-again Christian ballplayers believe that God grants eternal life to those who receive Jesus Christ.* The Bible says that only by faith in Christ — not through self-effort — can a person gain salvation. "For by grace you have been saved through faith; and that not of yourselves, it is a gift of God; not as a result of works, that no one should boast" (Ephesians 2:8,9). As former American League pitcher Geoff Zahn once said, "I [realized] that all my good deeds were worthless because they were on the outside, trying to make me look good, just like it said in the Bible. For example, I'd tell my fellow pitchers, 'Nice game,' when in my heart I was envious, hoping they would do poorly so I would look better and move ahead. Even though men are worthy of death, God sent His Son Jesus Christ to die for us and pay that penalty for our sins. I realized that the only way to heaven or everlasting life was to believe in what Jesus had already done for me."

●*Christian ballplayers seek to demonstrate love for others.* Black, white and Hispanic players worship together in chapel services throughout the major and minor leagues. This inter-racial fellowship is just one example of the love of Christ in baseball. Players are also taught in various situations — especially Professional Athletes Outreach conferences — how they can provide loving leadership for their wives and thus protect against the pressures that attack a pro athlete's marriage. Said Sharon Hargrove when her husband, Mike, was playing with the Cleveland Indians: "If baseball is on our list of priorities where it belongs — after God, each other and our family — then I usually can cope pretty well with what comes along."

●*Christian ballplayers acknowledge their imperfections.* "Christians aren't perfect, just forgiven," is a popular slogan, and it happens to express exactly what the Bible says. According to 1 John 1:8,9, "If we say that we have no sin, we are deceiving ourselves, and the truth is not in us. If we confess our sins, He is faithful and righteous to forgive us our sins and to cleanse us from all unrighteousness."

Yes, Christians have the power from the Holy Spirit to avoid sin, but no one correctly chooses to make use of that power all the time. National League pitcher John Denny, for example, has demonstrated the love of Christ in many situations, but he's the first to admit that his record is not 100 percent. Denny grew up in a broken home — his father left the family when John was young. John had seen little of his father over the years, but because of his growing faith he wanted to overcome his feelings of bitterness. Thus, he brought his dad in from Australia — while his mom and other family members gathered from within the States — to see him pitch in the 1983 World Series. A more beautiful picture of Christian love would be hard to imagine than Denny putting his arms around his father. "It was the power of the Lord working in me," says John.

But such a spiritual victory doesn't make the man exempt from sin. Denny has often wrestled with a strong temper, and he lost it in 1986 while playing for a slumping Cincinnati team. Removed from a losing effort against the Mets, Denny threw a bat at a TV cameraman who was recording his disappointment. Denny admits he has had a problem in dealing with the media, who he feels often treated him unfairly. "It's a problem, it's a real problem," said John in 1986, "and I do try to pray about it and I try to seek the Lord's will in it. But I know as I go through this roller coaster ride with the media, the good results that the Lord has in store will come through. In my situation with the media, if I [couldn't] turn it over to the Lord and trust in Him . . . then it would all be for nothing."

●*Christian ballplayers say their faith does not prohibit aggressive play.* Some people assume that a Christian will be weak, perhaps because they confuse the Christ-like quality of meekness (which means "power under control") with weakness. Asked about this very issue, Orel Hershiser laid his feelings on the line: "You don't have to be a wimp to be a Christian."

Actually, a proper view of the Christian faith should motivate the athlete to give his very best effort. The Bible says in Colossians 3:23, "Whatever you do, do your work heartily, as for the Lord rather than for men." In other words, the athlete should put his whole heart into his job — whether his manager, his teammates, and the fans are noticing — because he wants to please Christ through his effort. Tim Foli, a shortstop in both leagues prior to his retirement, said his Christian conversion led to an improved attitude on the field. "I still had my shortcomings, but I stopped blaming others for them," said Foli. "By accepting them [his weaknesses] myself, I became a better person. I used to spend a great deal of energy worrying about the fans, and what the writers wrote about me. I'd fight with umpires and other players. (Foli's nickname was "Crazy Horse.") Because of that, I was only able to give 60 to 70 percent of my ability to baseball."

But Foli received Christ at a Pro Athletes Outreach conference in February of 1978, then helped lead the Pirates to the 1979 World Series title. A career .250 hitter, Foli achieved a .291 mark for the Pirates that year.

●*Committed Christians in major league baseball can be examples to all of us in using their money for the good of others.* Never have baseball players been paid as highly as today, although athletes have always made big bucks and always will. (Even in 1930, Babe Ruth was asked about the fact that he made more money than President Herbert C. Hoover. Responded the Babe, "I had a better year than he did.") Each athlete, however, has the responsibility before God to use his money in a way that honors God.

Even before he'd finished one year in the big leagues, Andy Van Slyke had found a good financial model in John Denny. Said Van Slyke, "I'd like to be able to make a lot of money in investments and be able to use the money in a good way. I would like to give a lot back to the Lord's work. I would like to get into charity and things that would help spread the Word of God. Like something John Denny . . . did. He donated 250 acres of land to set up a camp for underprivileged kids. People who have money, not just ballplayers, should realize that it's not their money, it's the Lord's money."[1]

●*Christian ballplayers feel a responsibility to share their faith with other players in a sensitive fashion.* These baseball believers don't want to be preachy, but they do want to tell other players about the most important message in life. "[If] you develop friendships," said Bobby Richardson about his playing days, "you can show genuine concern, and that door will open."[2] Added Richardson on another occasion, "If someone had cancer and I had the cure, I would not just stand around and wait for the person to ask me for it. I would share the cure with him."[3] In the same way, committed Christians are eager to share the love of Jesus Christ.

●*The Christian movement in baseball has begun, in a more organized fashion than ever before, to reach out to the general public — both in North America and throughout the world.* Serving as a catalyst for this expanded outreach is Unlimited Potential, an organization located in Warsaw, Indiana, and directed by Tom Roy. Roy, formerly a pitcher in the San Francisco Giants' organization, founded Unlimited Potential in 1980.

The primary activity of Unlimited Potential is to hold evangelistic clinics, always in partnership with a local church and sometimes also with Baseball Chapel or another ministry. At such clinics, baseball coaches and players teach young boys the fundamentals of the game and, in another part of the program, relate how they met Christ. For example, one day in the spring of 1986, nine pros taught a clinic for 550 people at the University of Texas at Arlington. Scott Fletcher and Pete O'Brien of the Rangers spoke about their faith, and many in the crowd indicated personal interest in Jesus Christ. "We really care about these kids," says Roy, "and we feel we have something important to tell them."

Concerning other countries, Roy says, "There's so much baseball being played that doors are open all over the world." Nations which Unlimited Potential has visited include South Korea, Thailand, the Dominican Republic, the Philippines, Japan and Venezuela. A 1985 trip to Korea by Roy and the Astros' Glenn Davis was particularly memorable. They did clinics for high school and college teams and even for a Korean major league team. The Korean pros were awed to see Davis hit five or six straight rockets out of the park in batting practice, and they were also extremely open to the gospel message. Other Korean major league teams later expressed interest in having clinics in future years.

The players have responded with enthusiasm to Unlimited Potential clinics. "I've done a lot of baseball clinics before," said Bob Knepper, "but never one which had me share my faith at the conclusion. Unlimited Potential clinic outreach is fantastic and a wonderful way to reach children and adults."

* * *

The Christian movement in baseball has grown steadily, both in the numbers of players it has influenced and in the spiritual depth they show. Many inspiring stories could be told — in addition to those in this book — about the lives of past and present players who speak out for Christ. Chris Bando, Mike Moore, Mike Easler (an ordained Baptist minister), Kevin Bass, Jim Sundberg, Tony Fernandez, Paul Molitor, Terry Puhl, Darrell Porter, Craig Reynolds, Mike Davis, Tim Burke, Harold Reynolds, Tippy Martinez, Lee Tunnell, Jim Morrison, Larry Anderson, Darnell Coles and others could speak of their personal faith in the Savior.

But just one more story will summarize the struggles of the modern ballplayer and the joy he can find through Christ. Here's how Scott McGregor tells his personal saga of faith, beginning with his life in the '70s:

"When I was with friends, I was drinking and smoking dope; then when I saw the coach, I would say, 'I don't do that stuff.' I was living a double life. I was so wrapped in the pressures of the world that my pitching ability was disappearing . . .

"I thought that baseball would be my happiness. But what I saw began to shake the foundation of what was going to be my hope in life. I said to myself, 'This isn't it; there is more to life than this . . .'

"All the time, God was placing Christians along my way. When I joined the Baltimore Orioles, Pat Kelly was on the ball club and he had what I was looking for. I started attending chapel at the ball park on Sundays. The Word is preached there every Sunday for 20 minutes. My conversion wasn't an overnight thing — it took time; I meditated a lot. God knew the deep parts of my life. He knew those things happening inside me, and He knew how to get me.

"One day at the Bible study in the ball park, the

pastor asked if I could stay after the meeting, and I did. Time and time again, I had turned away from invitations to commit to the Lord. But that day, I stayed and I came to the Lord. I went home and told my wife about it. She started checking the Scriptures, and she gave her heart to the Lord, too . . .

"I wanted something better and I found something better. Now it's my duty to pass it on. God has taught me that I can never fulfill all the things I would like to do. I have to discern between the things He wants me to do and the things He doesn't want me to do.

"There is no way I could make it without Christ. I have found that being a Christian is a glorious 24-hour-a-day lifestyle. To anyone who wants a challenge, I say, 'Accept Jesus Christ as your Savior and start walking with Him. You'll be challenged every second of the day for the rest of your life.' "[4]

The former Yankee second baseman made history with a World Series grand slam. He enjoys telling the story — and using it to inspire others.

15

BOBBY RICHARDSON

My Grand Slam and Yours

*B*obby Richardson was never known for power hitting, unless perhaps the lack of it. In the Yankee lineup of the 1950s and 1960s, he was the one who didn't hit home runs, in contrast to such sluggers as Mickey Mantle, Roger Maris and Yogi Berra. Richardson instead helped the New Yorkers build a dynasty with his fine fielding and his hit-and-run ability.

But Richardson must have used somebody else's bat in the third game of the 1960 World Series against the Pirates. In the first inning, he belted a grand slam; then knocked in two more runs in the fourth. His six runs-batted-in for the game and 12 for the Series both set new records. Although the Pirates won the championship, Richardson was named Most Valuable Player.

Retired as a player since 1966, Richardson is baseball coach at Liberty University (Lynchburg, Virginia) and is president of Baseball Chapel.

* * *

No one was more surprised than I was when that ball flew out of Yankee Stadium for a grand slam in the third World Series game of 1960. Why? To start with, I'd hit only one home run that entire season. Next, I went to the plate with instructions to squeeze bunt, and it was only after I'd fouled off two pitches that I was allowed to swing away. Even then, however, I was just trying to hit the ball to the right side to keep from hitting into a double play.

Fortunately, I swung a little early at Clem Labine's pitch, and the ball headed toward the left fielder. When I rounded first base, I looked toward left field for the first time. Gino Cimoli had already gone to the fence and was looking down into his glove. I thought he had caught it, and there was a little sinking feeling in my heart.

Cimoli was looking into an empty glove. The ball had cleared the wall, and I experienced one of the top thrills of my career. I'll never forget circling the bases and then being greeted by three teammates who had also scored on just one swing of the bat. And to think that I was supposed to have bunted!

Not every grand slam takes place in a World Series game, but every grand slam is a breathtaking event. The impact of four runs on one play is overwhelming in a Little League or high school game just as in a big league game.

And that's why I'd like to describe an experience I've had in the Christian life by calling it a "spiritual grand slam." Allow me to tell you more about the time I personally received Jesus Christ as my Savior and Lord.

As a small boy, I went to church and Sunday school and memorized a lot of Scripture verses. I knew all about the story of Jesus Christ, but I did not know Him personally. One afternoon, at age 14, I talked with my pastor and suddenly realized that real Christianity didn't mean just living a good life. It meant that I must receive Christ as Lord and Savior of my life. So, that day I invited Christ into my life.

I call that experience a spiritual grand slam because it was the greatest event in my life. It introduced me to a God who loves me despite my weaknesses, who forgives my sins, who promises me eternal life. I simply cannot imagine going through life without His friendship and strength, and I'm sure the players who are profiled in this book would say the same. Fortunately, this same experience of knowing Christ personally can be shared by anyone who responds in faith to the following truths:

●*First, a spiritual grand slam is based on your awareness of God's love.* What kind of love does He have for you? An unconditional love, one that flows from Him regardless of your actions or attitudes. As the Bible puts it, "But God demonstrates His own love toward us, in that while we were yet sinners, Christ died for us" (Romans 5:8). It's also a love that has no limit. I say this because God was willing to send His own Son to die for us — that's how much He loves us. "For God so loved the world that He gave His only begotten Son, that whoever believes in Him should not perish but have eternal life" (John 3:16).

●*Second, a spiritual grand slam involves an understanding of sin.* If you packed 50,000 people into Yankee Stadium you could be sure that every single one of the 50,000 was sinful. How do I know? The Bible says, "all have sinned and fall short of the glory of God" (Romans 3:23). The result of sin is serious, to say the least. According to the Bible, "the wages of sin is death" (Romans 6:23). That means our sins bring with them a bitter payment — eternal separation from God — unless we find forgiveness.

●*Third, a spiritual grand slam requires an answer to the sin problem.* Fortunately, we are not required to supply that answer ourselves. That is what Jesus did when He died on the cross. Simply put, He took upon Himself our sins and accepted the wages for those sins through His own death. (See Matthew 20:28 and 1 Peter

2:24.) He rose again three days after His death, thus proving that He was and is the Son of God.

●*Fourth, a spiritual grand slam is possible only when we respond in faith to Jesus Christ.* We cannot reach God simply by attending church or doing good deeds, for these efforts cannot erase our sins. Instead, we must depend completely on Jesus for forgiveness. As the Bible says, "For by grace you have been saved through faith; and that not of yourselves, it is the gift of God; not as a result of works . . ." (Ephesians 2:8,9). In order to know Christ, a person must receive Him by faith. The Bible says, "But as many as received Him, to them He gave the right to become children of God, even to those who believe in His name" (John 1:12). Before I ever put on those Yankee pinstripes, I had to sign a contract with the team. The same is true with God — to be part of His family we must make a clearcut decision to trust Christ as Savior and Lord.

Perhaps you're wondering how you can be sure that Christ will respond to your faith. How will you know that He has forgiven you and come into your life? No, He won't necessarily give you the kind of goosebumps that go along with a grand slam in baseball. Instead, He offers something more reliable than emotions — His own promise to live within the heart of those who receive Him by faith. As Jesus said, "Behold, I stand at the door and knock; if anyone hears My voice and opens the door, I will come in to him" (Revelation 3:20).

If you understand and believe the things you've just read, I would suggest that you now trust Jesus to be your personal Savior. You can express your faith in prayer, which is simply talking with God. Your prayer should include the following thoughts:

1. Admit you are a sinner.

2. Thank God for sending His Son, Jesus Christ, to pay the penalty for your sins by dying on the cross.

3. Accept His forgiveness for your sins.

4. Ask Jesus to come into your life.

5. Express your willingness to allow Him to change your life so that you might live in a way that honors Him.

Why don't you take a minute right now to pray these things to God? This spiritual grand slam is a once-in-a-lifetime commitment, so make sure that you understand clearly what you've just read in this chapter.

* * *

Did you pray those thoughts to God with faith and sincerity? If you did, Jesus Christ entered your heart, bringing with Him forgiveness for your sins. You may or may not feel any different, but that's not important. Your new relationship with God is based on what Christ promised, not on how you feel.

If you did trust Jesus to be your Savior, you will soon observe changes in your attitudes and actions. As you saw in the ballplayers described in this book, these changes may affect your attitude toward yourself, your attitude toward relatives or friends, and even your purpose for life. (See 2 Corinthians 5:17.)

One final word. Just as a ballplayer functions best on a good team, so a Christian is only strong as part of a fellowship group. Make sure to become part of a church where Christ is honored and the Bible is clearly explained. The people in such a church can show you Christ's love and teach you how to follow Him.

I would also invite you to write to me so that I can send you materials to aid your spiritual growth. Please don't hesitate. I still remember the joy of my spiritual grand slam, and I'm eager to share in yours! Please write to:

> Bobby Richardson
> c/o Here's Life Publishers
> P.O. Box 1576
> San Bernardino, CA 92402-1576

Notes

Chapter 1
1. *Billy Sunday Speaks,* ed. Karen Gullen (New York: Chelsea House Publishers, 1970), p. 5.
2. William T. Ellis, *Billy Sunday — The Man and His Message* (Chicago: Moody Press, 1959) p. 32.
3. Ellis, p. 33.
4. Ellis, p. 94.
5. James C. Hefley, *Play Ball!* (Grand Rapids, MI: Zondervan, 1964) p. 27.
6. "Catch as Catch Can, II . . .," *Worldwide Challenge* (September 1978), p. 49.
7. Edward Kiersh, "Gary Carter: 'The Natural' Ticket to a Mets Pennant," *Inside Sports* (May 1985), p. 22.
8. "Andre's Astounding Prayer," *Worldwide Challenge* (December 1977), p. 48.

Chapter 13
1. Roger Kahn, *The Boys of Summer* (New York: Signet, 1973), p. 101.
2. *Current Biography 1945,* p. 498.
3. Murray Polner, *Branch Rickey* (New York: Signet, 1982), p. 240.
4. Jules Tygiel, *Baseball's Great Experiment* (New York: Vintage Books, 1984), p. 28.
5. Polner, p. 39-41.
6. Polner, p. 32.
7. Polner, p. 119.
8. Tygiel, p. 48.
9. Kahn, p. 357.
10. Polner, p. 165.
11. Fulton Oursler, "Rookie of the Year," *The Reader's Digest* (February 1948), p. 35.
12. Polner, p. 166-67.
13. Polner, p. 179.
14. Polner, p. 180.

15. Tygiel, p. 143.
16. Tygiel, p. 171.
17. Polner, p. 196.
18. Polner, p. 198.
19. Kahn, p. 299.
20. Polner, p. 199.
21. Polner, p. 201.
22. Tygiel, p. 200.
23. Polner, p. 205.
24. Tygiel, p. 343.
25. Polner, p. 60.

Chapter 14

1. Rick Hummel, "Supersub Andy Van Slyke," *St. Louis Post-Dispatch* (March 31, 1984), p. D-1.
2. Sara Anderson, "Bobby Richardson's Greatest Hits," *Athletes in Action* (Fall 1983), p. 46.
3. "A Coach With the Cure," *Athletes in Action* (1971), p. 34.
4. Scott McGregor, "God Set Me Free," *Decision* (April 1985), p. 4.